SELF-RIGHTEOUSNESS: OUR GREATEST DANGER

WHAT GOD SAYS AND DOES ABOUT THE RIGHTEOUSNESS OF SELF

Self-Righteousness:
Our Greatest Danger

What God Says and Does

About the Righteousness of Self

A Biblical Resource for Reality Checks That Includes Questions for Personal Reflection and Group Discussion and Informative Quotations From Dr. Martin Luther and Other Notable Writers

Charles T. Knippel, Ph.D.

Dedication

This book is dedicated to:

The Rev. Dr. David Fielding, pastor of Hope Lutheran Church in Granite City, Illinois, and his wife and partner in parish ministry, Connie.

———

My double first-cousin, Edward N. Johnson; his wife, Vicki; and their son, Charles Edward.

———

My brothers-in-law, Donald L. Niehaus and Daniel W. Niehaus.

Copyright © 2007 by Charles Taylor Knippel
263 Oakley Place
East Alton, Illinois 62024

All rights reserved. No part of this publication may be reproduced, stored in a retrieval system, or transmitted, in any form or by any means electronic, mechanical, photocopying, recording, or otherwise, without the prior written permission by Charles T. Knippel unless noted.

ISBN 978-0-6151-5879-2

ACKNOWLEDGEMENTS

All quotations used in this book for which this page and the Notes do not cite a permission to quote are in the public domain or considered as fair usage. The source of the graphics is Microsoft Word 2003 used by the author in the preparation of this book.

All scripture quotations, unless otherwise indicated, are taken from the Holy Bible, New International Version®. NIV®. Copyright © 1973, 1978, 1984 by International Bible Society. Used by permission of Zondervan. All rights reserved.

Excerpts from *Luther's Works Vols. 6, 7, 9, 12, 16, 17, 25, 26, 27,* respectively, © 1970, 1965, 1960, 1955, 1969, 1972, 1972, 1963, 1964 by Concordia Publishing House. Used with permission. All rights reserved.

Excerpts from *What Luther Says Vol. 3* © 1959, 1987 by Concordia Publishing House. Used with permission. All rights reserved.

Quotations from vols. 37, 44, and 51 of *Luther's Works*, American Edition, edited by Robert H. Fischer, James Atkinson, John W. Doberstein, respectively, copyright © 1961 by Muhlenberg Press. Reproduced by permission of Augsburg Fortress.

Quotations from *The Book of Concord*, edited by Theodore G. Tappert, copyright © 1959 by Fortress Press. Reproduced by permission of Augsburg Fortress.

++++++

To the Rev. Dr. David Fielding, my highly esteemed colleague and pastor, I express my deepest gratitude for his invaluable suggestions and editorial assistance. He has generously given his time, knowledge, and wisdom to this book.

Heartfelt thanks to my dear wife, Donna, for her encouragement and support and for her nearby presence during my many hours at the computer.

To God be praise and glory through Jesus Christ forever and ever!

Contents

Preface	15
Introduction	17
Part 1 Our Greatest Danger: What God Says About Self-righteousness	**21**
1. A Reality of Life	21
A Reality Check for a Dangerous Reality	21
A Reality with Identity	21
Look at the Pharisees	23
Jesus Speaks	26
St. Paul's Conviction	29
2. A Reality Before God	31
Pharisaic Attitude	31
According to St. Paul	31

The Witness of Reformers	32
3. A Reality Among People	35
Pharisaic Examples	35
Exhibited by Jesus' Disciples	36
St. Paul's Observations	37
What Reformers Say	38
4. Our Greatest Danger Before God	41
Teachings of Jesus	41
St. Paul's Affirmation	41
Opposed by the Reformers	43
5. Our Greatest Danger Among People	45
Danger to Ourselves	45
Danger to Others	46
6. Unrecognized by the Self-righteous	51
7. Its Origins and Dynamics	53
Origins of Self-righteousness	53
Dynamics of Self-righteousness	56

Part 2 Our Greatest Danger: What God Does About Self-righteousness — 59

8. Shows Us Our Need and Inability to Rescue Ourselves From Self-righteousness — 59

9. Gives Us True Righteousness Before Him — 63

    God's Gift — 63

    God's Declaration for Jesus' Sake — 65

    Obtained Through Faith in Jesus — 68

10. Gives Us True Righteousness Among Others — 73

    Characterized by Humility — 73

    Modeled and Empowered by Jesus — 74

    Requires True Self-Esteem — 76

11. Enables Us to Walk the Path to Righteousness Before God and Among Others — 77

    God's Law Calls All People to Repentance (contrition) — 77

    The Gospel Calls for the Faith of Repentance from All People — 79

God Calls All Christians to the Life of Repentance (contrition and faith) 79

Reasons for the Invasion of Self-righteousness into Christian Lives 83

God Gives Us an Example of Repentance (contrition and faith), Forgiveness, and Renewal though Faith 86

The Path to the Life of Repentance (contrition and faith) is the Christian's Daily Return to the Baptismal Font Enabled and Nurtured by the Gospel in Word and Sacrament 86

The Path to Righteousness Among Others is the Life of Repentance (contrition and faith) 92

12. Calls Us to Do Reality Checks 93

13. Bids to Help Others 97

Biblical Reflections 97

　　　　Contemporary Illustrations

　　　　　　A Conversation with a Non-Christian

　　　　　　A Conversation Between Christian
　　　　　　Friends

　　　　　　A Conversation Between Engaged Christians

Conclusion											113

Appendix: Questions To Promote Focused Reflection and
　　　Discussion										117
Notes											139

ABBREVIATIONS

LW — Luther, Martin. *Luther's Works.* American Edition. General editors Jaroslav Pelikan and Helmut T. Lehmann. 56 vols. St. Louis: Concordia, and Philadelphia: Muhlenberg and Fortress, 1955-1986. (Wherever possible I have taken my selected Luther quotes from the American Edition of *Luther's Works.* Otherwise, I have quoted Luther as translated in volume 3 of *What Luther Says* by Ewald Plass.)

Plass — Plass, Ewald M. compil. *What Luther Says: An Anthology.* Vol. 3, *Prayers to Zeal, Index.* St. Louis: Concordia, 1959.

Tappert — Tappert, Theodore G., ed. *The Book of Concord.* Philadelphia: Fortress Press, 1959.

PREFACE

Beware of danger! A danger is someone or something that can or does cause us harm. We view various people and a variety of things as dangerous to our well-being. Among serious dangers are viruses; diseases; amoral, immoral, and dishonest people; terrorists; and other armed enemies intent on our destruction. Sometimes we are our own worst danger.

To speak of a danger as our *greatest* is to say that such a danger threatens to cause us the greatest possible harm. To speak of a danger as the greatest is to indicate that there is one danger more dangerous than all other dangers. Of all dangers, we are to beware most of all of the greatest danger.

In this book I contend that there is indeed a greatest danger. I mean that it is the ultimate or most extreme danger. It is the worst of the worst. This is not a belief that I have invented. It is the teaching of the Bible and therefore the verdict of God.

What then, according to God, is the greatest danger for us humans? God says it is self-righteousness. Self-righteousness is our greatest danger both before God and among people. It is the worst of the worst in life. We are to beware of this extreme hazard.

Throughout the pages of this book I review what God, in His Word and through people guided by His Word, says to expose self-righteousness as our gravest danger, to reveal to us the true righteousness that rescues us from all the evils of self-righteousness, and to show us how to deal with the insidious and mysterious inroads of self-righteousness into our lives and the lives of others. In this book we ponder ways to beware of, and be rid of, the greatest danger.

By examining what God says and does about self-righteousness, we come to realize the necessity of reality checks for our extreme danger. Thus this book provides the understandings we need to make necessary and continuous reality checks and to embrace God's way of escape.

We look to God to bless us with the best of the best for the worst of the worst as we attend to God's words of Law and Gospel.

INTRODUCTION

In His Word, called the Bible and the Sacred Scripture, God has much to say about the identity and dangers of self-righteousness and the identity and benefits of the true righteousness that is acceptable before Him and beneficial to us and others. God's Word is the primary and authoritative source for our pursuit.

In the 16th century self-righteousness was a high profile topic. The discussion of self-righteousness was front and center in the reforming ministry of Martin Luther. He and other theologians of his time spoke and wrote about its dangers. They earnestly urged people to turn from the self-righteousness from which God rescues us and to the true righteousness for which God rescues us.

Today, as in past ages, self-righteousness continues to be the greatest danger for us and everyone. We can aptly say that self-righteousness is not simply a danger for us. In actuality, as we have already affirmed, it is the *greatest* danger for us as we live both before God and among people. Today the discussion of self-righteousness may employ somewhat different language, but it is very much the same. We talk about arrogance, haughtiness, egotism, narcissism, intolerance, prejudice, and the obsessive need to control people and situations. When we do, we are simply talking about different faces of the prideful righteousness of self.

Because self-righteousness is extremely perilous for us and others, it is urgent for us to understand the origin and nature of self-righteousness and to discover how its insidious and surreptitious perils express themselves. We desperately need to examine ourselves fearlessly for self-righteousness by way of reality checks as we live out our lives before God and among others. At the same time, it is absolutely imperative for us to know about God's actions to rescue us from the righteousness of self and to make it possible for us to possess His true saving and life-changing righteousness. Thus, as promised in the Preface, in this book we will consider what God has to say to us in His Word about self-righteousness and what He does about self-righteousness. Our intention is to prepare ourselves and others to beware of self-righteousness and make much-needed reality checks for overcoming our greatest danger by the grace and guidance of God. In fact, every section of this book is itself a resource for making reality checks as we read the book and refer to the book in the days that follow.

In our investigative pursuit we will add to our anticipated study of Holy Scripture a review of helpful insights offered by dedicated students of the Bible, especially Dr. Martin Luther, the great theologian and reformer of the sixteenth century. As a learned and competent interpreter of Holy Scripture and observer of human behavior, Luther dealt vigorously with the critical problem of self-righteousness. He taught and warned people of world and church about the dangers of the righteousness of self. By God's leading, he restored to the world and church a right understanding of the true and only righteousness that prevails before

God, changes and enhances our lives, and enables us to enrich the lives of others. He boldly proclaimed God's rescue from self-righteousness. We will give a considerable amount of attention to what Luther has to say.

To give readers the opportunity to reflect upon and discuss the content of this book with one another, I have provided questions for personal consideration and mutual conversation. I intend these resources to be helpful for both individuals and study-discussion groups.

In the preparation of this book, I have written for persons in all walks of life and for ministers of God's people for their own personal reflection and for use in caring for and serving people. With this in mind I have sought to use language readily meaningful to people of various ages and a variety of vocations.

When organizing and writing this book, I have sought to be clear and logical in unfolding our topic and discussing its various facets. As a result of this intention and because of the seriousness of the subject, I am sometimes repetitious for the sake of clarity and emphasis and often of necessity because so many topics are overlapping in thought. I decided that much of what I want to share warrants repetition in various contexts especially because this book is designed not only for continuous reading but also to be used from time to time for reflection and discussion of its various sections and topics. Thus I lay claim to the Latin proverb, *"Repetitio est mater studiorum."* ("Repetition is the mother of learning.") Stay with me, and I believe you will find blessings I have discovered in writing this book. God bless us, each and everyone, with Jesus' righteousness that enables us to stand holy and boldly before God as His forgiven people and to live righteously among people.

Before we move to Chapter 1, I wish to add a word about a personal concern I have about this book. In writing this book I don't want to be self-righteous in any way in my presentation. Nor do I want to sound self-righteous. I realize how difficult it is to write about self-righteousness without crossing the thin line between speaking the truth in love and speaking the truth in loveless and critical ways. If I should cross that line, I ask God and you for forgiveness. I assure you that I first speak to myself, and only then to you who read, as I write about the ultimate danger of self-righteousness before God and among people. I ask God to enable me to speak the truth in love that we may all possess the righteousness that God gives and grow in faith and life in Jesus Christ.

Part 1

Our Greatest Danger: What God Says About Self-righteousness

1. A Reality of Life

A Reality Check for a Dangerous Reality

The self-righteousness of which we speak is a dangerous realism. It calls for serious and exacting reality checks on the part of both Christians and non-Christians. It affects us and every human being. As we shall show time and again, the greatest danger is so insidious and surreptitious that to recognize it we must clearly understand what it is and how it works. Then, we need to realistically examine ourselves and our lifestyles to determine if, how, and to what extent the dangerous reality destructively works in us and through us.

A Reality with Identity

At the outset, it is absolutely essential for us to affirm that self-righteousness is a phenomenon that truly exists among us and is not a figment of our imagination. This is important because self-righteousness is not readily recognized by the self-righteous person. It is the master of deceit and obfuscation. Sometimes it is clearly observable to others by the attitudes and actions of the self-righteous. At other times it is cleverly hidden from others as it is to every self-righteous person.

What is the self-righteousness of which we speak and of which we are to beware? What is this righteousness of self that is such a grave and extreme danger? Here is the answer: Self-righteousness before God is our belief that we are good enough and do enough good to obtain and possess God's favor. Self-righteousness among people is our haughty belief that we are superior to other people and can manipulate and use them for our selfish purposes and to their detriment.

Self-righteousness, sinful pride, and arrogance are closely related, and the concepts are often used synonymously and interchangeably. They are interrelated companions rooted deeply in our inherited sinfulness. Throughout these pages I speak of self-righteousness as a manifestation or expression of sinful pride or as emerging from sinful pride that is traditionally identified by theologians as the primary sin. I view self-righteousness as producing, in turn, a haughty mindset and generating arrogant actions in the face of God and people. In a subsequent chapter we will think more about the origins and deceptive dynamics of self-righteousness. However, at this point I do want to note than when speak of pride, I am talking about sinful pride in contrast to legitimate, healthy, and humble pride that expresses personal satisfaction and pleasure from a particular source, especially from something accomplished or a quality possessed. As an example, St. Paul wrote of the Corinthians, "I have great confidence in you; I take pride in you" (2 Corinthians 7:4).

Look at the Pharisees

In the New Testament the Pharisees demonstrate the reality of self-righteousness in people's lives and serve as examples of self-righteousness. With clarity they show us what self-righteousness is and how it works detrimentally in human lives.

The Pharisees were one group of religious leaders, probably 6000 to 7000 in number, among the Jewish people at the time of Jesus. They were devoted to living scrupulously according to their understanding of God's Law, the ceremonial laws of Moses, and the traditions added by their forefathers. Emphasizing the observance of traditional rites and ceremonies, they believed that religion consisted primarily in externally and formally observing what the Old Testament laws and traditions required (Matthew 15:6-9). These Pharisees loved to be praised by others. They wore special garments and took the most important seats when they attended synagogue services and special banquets and celebrations (Matthew 23:5-7).

In general, the Pharisees were considered by their contemporaries to be decent and upright people who were well-respected in Jewish society. Some, like Nicodemus, were obviously more devoted than some to the true meaning and observance of God's Word.

What made the Pharisees unacceptable to Jesus was the way they as a group officially understood their outward and scrupulous observance of Old Testament laws and the traditions of the fathers. Tragically, they believed that simply "going through the motions" to keep laws and traditions made them dearly loved by God and better than others. Going through outward actions to fulfill Old Testament laws and the traditions of the fathers caused Pharisees to overlook the inner meaning of God's law summarized in the Ten Commandments—love for God and love for others. This led them in actuality to disobey the inner meaning and intent of God's law. In short, the Pharisees, for the most part, were proudly self-righteous.

The account of Jesus' interaction with the Pharisees in Mark chapter 7 exposes the theological position of the Pharisees. Mark gives us the details.

> The Pharisees and some of the teachers of the law who had come from Jerusalem gathered around Jesus and saw some of his disciples eating food with hands that were unclean, that is, unwashed. (The Pharisees and all the Jews do not eat unless they give their hands a ceremonial washing, holding to the tradition of the elders. When they come from the marketplace, they do not eat unless they wash. And they observe many other traditions, such as the washing of cups, pitchers, and kettles.) So the Pharisees and teachers of the law asked Jesus, "Why don't your disciples live according to the tradition of the elders instead of eating their food with 'unclean' hands?" He replied, "Isaiah was right when he prophesied about you hypocrites, as it is written: 'These people honor me with their lips, but their hearts are far from me. They worship me in vain; their teachings are but rules taught by men. You have let go of the commands of God and are holding on to the traditions of men." And he said to them: "You have a fine way of setting aside the commands of God in order to observe your own traditions! . . . Thus you nullify the word of

God by your tradition that you have handed down." (Mark 7:1-9, 13)

We see the reality of self-righteousness at work in the lives of the Pharisees in their persistent opposition to Jesus during the days of His ministry. Jesus was not the kind of political messianic person these Pharisees expected to free the Jewish people from the oppression of Roman rule. They believed that Jesus and His disciples were not rightly devoted to God's laws and the traditions of the fathers (Matthew 15:1-10). They saw Jesus and His disciples as threats to their religious beliefs and practices and their place in society.

The Pharisees sought to discredit Jesus and ascribed His miracles to Satan's power (Matthew 12:22-24). They criticized Him and His disciples for not keeping the Sabbath as they thought it should be kept (Matthew 12:1-13). Time after time they tried to trap Jesus to show that He was wrong in what He said and did in order to get Him into trouble with the people and the Romans in change of Palestine (Matthew 22:15-22). They frequently condemned Jesus and His disciples for associating with sinners (Luke 15:1-2). They accused Jesus of blasphemy for claiming to be God's Son and the Promised One and for claiming that He had authority to forgive sins (Luke 5:17-26). Finally, together with other Jewish leaders, the Pharisees planned to destroy Jesus, had Him arrested, and saw to it that the Roman governor put Him to death by crucifixion (John 11:45-53). In short, the Pharisees wanted to be rid of this man who criticized and condemned them as self-righteous, who claimed to be God's promised Messiah, and who threatened to undermine their position of authority among the people. Self-righteousness was very real in the daily lives of the Pharisees. Their lives indisputably showed that self-righteousness exists in the lives of human beings.

Jesus Speaks

Jesus Himself attested to the existence of self-righteousness in the lives of people by disclosing and speaking against the self-righteousness of the Pharisees. He had much to say to the Pharisees and about them. He told them they were wrong when they gave outward compliance to the traditions of the fathers an importance above God's laws and their true meaning. They were gravely mistaken, he testified, when they trusted in their own supposed goodness for a saving relationship with God (Matthew 15:1-9, Matthew 5:20, Luke 18:9-14). A number of times Jesus called them blind guides of the people (Mathew 23:16). He spoke of them as hypocrites, as people who pretended to be better that they actually were. Jesus called the Pharisees snakes and a brood of vipers (Matthew 23). He compared them to "whitewashed tombs which look beautiful on the outside but on the inside are full of dead men's bones and everything unclean" (Matthew 23:27).

Jesus told His disciples to beware of adopting the hypocritical ways of the Pharisees (Luke 12:1-3). He assured them that claiming righteousness like the Pharisees would lead them to condemnation (Matthew 5:20). Both Matthew and Luke recorded powerful and penetrating "woes" that Jesus spoke against the Pharisees (Matthew 23:13-29; Luke 11:42-52). They are telling statements that compel our attention.

Two parables that Jesus spoke tell us much about the Pharisees and clarify Jesus' attitude toward them. The first is the "Parable of the Pharisee and the Tax Collector" (Luke 18:9-11). Both the Pharisee and the tax collector went into the temple to pray. The Pharisee stood up and prayed about himself. He thanked God that he was not like other men, a robber, an evil doer, an adulterer, and certainly not like the tax collector standing nearby. He bragged before God that he fasted twice a week and gave a tithe of all he got. The tax collector, however, in contrast to the Pharisee, beat on his chest and didn't feel worthy even to look heavenward. To God he cried out, "God, have mercy on me, a sinner."

Luke comments that Jesus told this parable to people who were confident of their own righteousness. At the conclusion of the parable Jesus said of the tax collector, "I tell you that this man, rather than the other one, went home justified before God" (Luke 18:14). Self-righteousness doesn't get us in good with God. It doesn't justify us before God; it condemns us.

The second parable is the "Parable of the Lost Son" that Jesus told to Pharisees and teachers of the law (Luke 15:11-31). I'm sure you remember it well. There was a man who had two sons. Upon the insistence of the younger son, who wanted to strike out on his own and travel to a distant country, the father divided his property between his two sons—the younger, who went far from home, and the older, who stayed at home.

After the younger son, far away from home, had spent his wealth on wild living and had to take care of pigs and eat their food (an unthinkable thing for a Jewish person), he decided to return home and throw himself on the mercy of his father. You will remember that when he was close to home, the father ran down the road to embrace and kiss him. Even though, admitting his sin, the son declared that he no longer deserved to be a son, the father gave him a fine robe, a ring for his finger, and shoes for his feet. Then he arranged for a feast to celebrate his son's return. The younger son was very much like the tax collector in the temple. Sorry for his grave sins, he penitently asked for mercy.

The older son is the Pharisee figure in the parable. When he came upon the feast and the celebration, he was angry and refused to join the festivities even though the father pleaded with him. He complained bitterly about his father's goodness, claiming that he, the obedient and hardworking son, had never been given such an extravagant party. To this the father replied, "You are always with me, and everything I have is yours. But we had to celebrate and be glad because this brother of yours was dead and is alive again; he was lost and is found" (Luke 15:31).

The older son was very much a Pharisee in his behavior. He believed that the father "owed him" because he was so good, and he looked down on his brother whom he viewed as unworthy of the Father's love and generosity. The older son suffered from self-righteousness. He shows us how self-righteousness can cause us to be.

In dealing with the Pharisees Jesus exposed the reality of self-righteousness as an integral part of the human condition. It is evident and cannot be denied.

St Paul's Conviction

St. Paul, himself a Pharisee before he became a Christian, wrote prolifically about self-righteousness in his New Testament letters. In his letter to the Romans, he spoke of the righteousness of self of many of his Jewish brothers and sisters. He wrote of them, "Since they did not know the righteousness that comes from God and sought to establish their own, they did not submit to God's righteousness" (Romans 10:3). Paul's Israelite brothers and sisters sought to establish their own righteousness, and St. Paul ministered to them for their liberation from this extreme peril.

Self-righteousness among the members of congregations to whom St. Paul wrote continually threatened his message and work. Thus St. Paul reminded his fellow-Christians, and reminds us too, that the Law of God written across the pages of the Scripture and also in human hearts declares that we and all human beings are unrighteous before God. We are sinners who deserve God's punishment now and forever. We are born sinful and all sorts of disobedient thoughts, feelings, and actions erupt from our unrighteous sinful nature (Romans 3:10-20; Galatians 5:19-21; Ephesians 2:1).

There can be no mistake: St. Paul teaches the reality of self-righteousness and that we have no righteousness of our own. We have no reason at all to believe that there is something good in us that makes us acceptable to God and better than other people. Yet, the very nature of sin that lives in everyone causes the attitude of self-righteousness again and again to rear its ugly head in our lives. Sin, by its very nature, seeks to allure us in very subtle and deceptive ways to be self-righteous—to believe that we can, at least to some extent, earn or deserve God's love and acceptance. This enticement of the sin of pride is manifested in self-righteousness and is powerful and ever-present. It demands our most serious and earnest kind of reality checks (Galatians 1:6-9, 3:1-14). Self-righteousness is a real fact of life and a real force operative, to some degree or another, in the life of each one of us.

2. A Reality Before God

Pharisaic Attitude

Self-righteousness is a reality that faces in two directions. First of all, it is a reality before God. It is our most perilous danger before God.

The Pharisees are the embodiment of the reality of self-righteousness before God. Jesus' parable of the Pharisee and tax collector in the temple is a telling example of this. The Pharisee was clearly self-righteousness before God.

How did the Pharisee demonstrate his "before God" self-righteousness? The Pharisee told God how good a person he was. He wasn't a robber, an evildoer, an adulterer, or a bad person like the tax collector also praying in the temple. As a matter of fact, he fasted twice a week and gave a tithe of everything he obtained.

Obviously, the Pharisee believed he was "in good with God" because of how virtuous he was. He disclosed his self-righteousness when "he *stood up* and prayed *about himself*" (Luke 18:11; *my emphasis*). The Pharisee showed no humility at all before God. In reality, he demanded love and respect from God as a reward for his goodness.

According to St. Paul

St. Paul addressed the issue of self-righteousness before God. Writing to the Romans, St. Paul affirmed, "No one will be declared righteous in his [God's] sight by observing the law; . . ." (Romans 3:20). By these words he indicated that there are those who want to be seen as righteous in God's sight by their observance of the law.

In his letter to the Galatians Paul also talked about people "who rely on observing the law" (Galatians 3:10) and are trying to be justified by keeping the law (Galatians 5:4). St. Paul was characterizing people who sought to be righteous before God by keeping the law. These people believed that they could be good enough and do enough good to earn or merit God's favor. They were blatantly self-righteous before God.

The Witness of Reformers

Dr. Martin Luther spoke and wrote extensively about self-righteousness before God. In his commentary on Psalm 51, Luther spoke of the proud and self-righteous. He observed that they "do not want to be known as sinners and cannot stand it if anyone condemns their Pharisaic righteousness."[1] In the same commentary, he observed that the "idea of self-righteousness is the bitterest blasphemy against God."[2]

Lecturing on the book of the prophet Isaiah, Luther had this to say about self-righteousness before God: "[T]he ungodly self-righteous shape God according to their own worship and prescribe for themselves a god according to their own opinion."[3] In comments on Galatians 5:3, Luther observed, "[T]he self-righteous, who refrain from sins outwardly and seem to live blameless and religious lives, cannot avoid a presumption of confidence and righteousness, which cannot coexist faith in Christ."[4]

Like Luther, John Calvin, another 16th century reformer, taught the existence of the self-righteous nature of people before God. He spoke of people who desire to become right with God by their own merits or works. Calvin asserted, "Those who say they will be justified by their merits, or 'meritorious works' as they call them, have they not been driven to excessive pride by the devil?"[5] In a sermon titled "Justification by Grace" Calvin observed that among many the righteousness of self is commonly believed. He commented, "[H]owever much it may be commonly held that a good man can earn favor and acceptance with God, men are very seriously mistaken in such matters."[6]

Like both Luther and Calvin, John Wesley was cognizant from his biblical studies of the human person's proclivity to trust in the righteousness of self to stand before God. In a sermon on "The Righteousness of Faith," he proclaimed, "How many who have now a 'zeal for God,' yet have it not 'according to knowledge;' but are still seeking 'to establish their own righteousness,' as the ground of their pardon and acceptance; and therefore, vehemently refuse to 'submit themselves unto the righteousness of God!'"[7]

3. A Reality Among People

Pharisaic Examples

Self-righteous people are not only self-righteous before God but also among people. Luke writes that people who are confident of their own righteousness look down on others (Luke 18:9). Self-righteous people think they are better than other people and typically abuse them in a variety of ways. Some ways are quite noticeable; others are not so readily apparent. There are people, of course, who say that what we consider to be self-righteousness is merely self-confidence, assertiveness, and competitiveness. There may be a godly kind of self-confidence, assertiveness, and competitiveness but only too often these behaviors are expressions of self-righteousness that foster self-aggrandizement and diminish and destroy the lives of others.

The Pharisees saw themselves as quite godly, but they were negative forces in the lives of many people. From their self-righteous stance Pharisees abused Jesus. A review of some facts, we noted earlier, show this clearly. The Pharisees criticized Him and His disciples for actions they considered unacceptable, tried to entrap Him, accused Him of blasphemy and of being in league with the devil, helped take Him captive, condemned Him to death on trumped up changes, insisted that the Roman governor put Him to death, and saw to it that He was crucified as a common criminal. Quite likely they were among the Jewish leaders who bribed the soldiers at the risen Jesus' empty tomb to say that His disciples had taken His body away.

From the New Testament record we discover that Pharisees neglected their parents. Jesus said to them, "'But you say that if a man says to his father or mother, "Whatever help you might otherwise have received from me is a gift devoted to God," he is not to "honor His father" with it. Thus you nullify the word of God for the sake of your tradition. You hypocrites'" (Matthew 15:4-7)! The Pharisees insisted that their gift to God excused them taking care of their parents.

Jesus also said of the Pharisees that they "neglected the more important matters of the law—justice, mercy and faithfulness." To them He said,

Woe to you, teachers of the law and Pharisees, you hypocrites! You give a tenth of your spices—mint, ill, and cumin. But you have neglected the more important matters of the law—justice, mercy and faithfulness. You should have practiced the latter without neglecting the former. (Matthew 23:23)

From the Gospel accounts we learn that Pharisees very likely would have prevented Jesus from healing the man with the shriveled hand on the Sabbath day (Matthew 12:9-14). It seems certain that they would have stoned the woman caught in the act of adultery if Jesus had not intervened (John 8:1-11). The Pharisees' self-righteousness was the guiding principle of their lives.

Exhibited by Jesus' Disciples

Jesus' own disciples sometimes exhibited self-righteousness in their relationships with others. One day Jesus and His disciples traveled through a Samaritan village. The people of that village did not welcome

Jesus because they knew He was going to Jerusalem, and they didn't like the Jews. The disciples James and John reacted to the situation and self-righteously said to Jesus, "Lord, do you want us to call fire down from heaven to destroy them?" Jesus was displeased with their arrogant attitude toward "the others" of the Samaritan village, and He rebuked James and John. (Luke 9:51-56)

Then, there was another self-righteous day in the life of James and John. They presumptuously came to Jesus and asked to be given positions above the other disciples. They asked Jesus to let them sit on his right hand and left hand in glory. Jesus replied that those "places belong to those for whom they have been prepared." He then took opportunity to teach that greatness comes through service. The other ten disciples were impacted by the request of James and John. "When the ten heard about this, they became indignant with James and John." (Mark 10:35-41)

St. Paul's Observations

In his letter to the Philippians St. Paul recognized that self-righteousness directs itself toward others. He wrote, "Do nothing out of selfish ambition and conceit, but in humility consider others better than yourself. Each of you should look not only to your own interests, but also to the interests of others better than yourselves" (Philippians 2:3-4). The self-righteous, by virtue of their self-righteous stance, are selfishly ambitious and conceited. They look only to their own interests and are not concerned about the interests of others who go without their care.

Self-righteous people think highly of themselves in interpersonal relationships. Paul wrote, "Do not think of yourselves more highly than you ought, but rather think of yourself with sober judgment, in accordance with the measure of faith God has given you" (Romans 12:3). It is by sober judgment, St. Paul implies, that we are able to carry out God's design for His Church that "in Christ we who are many form one body, and each member belongs to all the others" (Romans 12: 3-5). Thus he went on to write, "Live in harmony with one another. Do not be proud. But be willing to associate with people of low position. Do not be conceited" (Romans 12:16).

What Reformers Say

In his commentary on the Book of Genesis Luther points to Laban's behavior as self-righteous and to his words and actions toward Jacob as expressions of his self-righteousness. Luther speaks of Laban as a "very cunning and self-righteous man" whose self-righteousness affected others. Of Laban Luther wrote, "[T]o promote his own glory and to defend his own righteousness, he finds fault with Jacob that his own wrath might not seem to have been empty and without strength and that Jacob in terror might confess his sin. This is what the proud hypocrite and very cunning and self-righteous man wanted." [1]

Martin Luther emphatically viewed self-righteous persons as disturbing the lives of those about them. In his 1535 preface to his commentary on Galatians, he wrote about how self-righteousness caused the people of Israel to harm others. He observed that "[S]atan, that is, the insane idea of self-righteousness made such headway among them that they killed all the prophets and finally even their promised Messiah. . . ."[2]

In his writings John Calvin observes that self-righteous people are self-righteous among other people. For example, he speaks of us as being full of corruption, filth, and uncleanness. Calvin writes: "[G]od finds us void of all goodness; we have not one drop of virtue, wisdom, or righteousness, but contrariwise, we are full of corruption; we are ready to burst for filth and uncleanness. . . ."[3] People with no righteousness and full of corruption, filth, and uncleanness are obviously self-righteous among people as well as before God.

That prideful self-righteousness has to do with interpersonal relationships was the contention of John Wesley. In a sermon titled "The Deceitfulness of the Human Heart," Wesley preached:

> When Satan had once transfused his own self-will and pride into the parents of mankind, together with a new species of sin,—love of the world, the loving the creature above the Creator,—all manner of wickedness soon rushed in; all ungodliness and with all manner of abominations; unrighteousness; shooting out into crimes of every kind; soon covering the whole face of the earth with all manner of abominations.[4]

Self-righteousness is real and endangers and diminishes human life.

4. Our Greatest Danger Before God

Teachings of Jesus

Self-righteousness before God is not only an actuality; it is the *greatest danger* before God. In the Sermon on the Mount Jesus told His hearers that they would not enter the kingdom of heaven unless their righteousness surpassed that of the scribes and Pharisees (Matthew 5:20). Jesus clearly declared that self-righteous persons cannot enter the kingdom of God. He proclaimed:

> I tell you the truth, the tax collectors and the prostitutes are entering the kingdom of heaven ahead of you. For John came to show you the way of righteousness and you did not believe him, but the tax collectors and the prostitutes did. And even after you saw this, you did not repent and believe him. (Matthew 21:31-32)

In the words of J.B. Phillips, "[Jesus] was sudden death to pride, pomposity, and pretence."[1]

St Paul's Affirmation

St. Paul wrote about the dangers of self-righteousness before God, especially in his letter to the Romans. In this letter St. Paul contrasts self-righteousness with the righteousness that God credits to unrighteous persons who repent of their sins and through faith accept Jesus as their Savior from sin, death, and eternal condemnation.

St. Paul told the Christians in Rome that no one will be declared righteous in God's sight by observing the law (Romans 3:19). St. Paul was definite in saying that absolutely no one can claim to be righteous before God. There is no room for self-righteousness in anyone's life. Paul writes, "We have already made the charge that Jews and Gentiles alike are all under sin. As it is written, 'There is no one righteous, not even one, there is no one who understands, no one who seeks God. All have turned away, they have together become worthless; there is no one who does good, not even one'...." (Romans 3:9-12). St. Paul went on to say:

> Now we know that whatever the law says, it says to those who are under the law, so that every mouth may be silenced and the whole world accountable to God. Therefore no one will declared righteous in his sight by observing the law; rather through the law we become conscious of sin. (Romans 3:19-20)

Beware of self-righteousness. For us, any of us, to cling to the notion that we have some kind of righteousness of self that puts us into a right relationship with God is wrong, foolish, extremely hazardous, and spiritually suicidal. Surely, we can understand why self-righteousness is the worst danger before God. Such folly results only in death now and hereafter. It prevents people from hearing and paying attention to the Gospel of God's undeserved favor in His Son Jesus. After all, they believe they have no need for God's mercy and forgiveness. They see themselves already acceptable to God by virtue of their own supposed goodness and merit. How sad because we have nothing, absolutely nothing, to offer God for Him to embrace us! How sad because "the wages of sin is death" (Romans 6:23). Luther said it succinctly, "Although external vices, adultery, fornication, theft, are also hindrances in the way of the Lord which must be removed, yet presumption and self-righteousness are far greater and graver; for they absolutely preclude the approach to grace."[2]

Opposed by the Reformers

Martin Luther understood and taught that righteousness of self before God is the extreme danger. In his remarks about Joseph's brothers, when they unknowingly met Joseph in Egypt, Luther said:

> This is indeed the fruit of self-righteousness, which makes men smug and stubborn, especially in the case of the monks and the Baalites, who are not simply foolish and lacking in mental power but are afflicted with madness and insanity, with which they arrogate to themselves such great purity and innocence that they do not want to creep on the ground, as sinners usually do, but have the audacity to put their heads among the clouds. Therefore they are hurled down to the depths of hell by God's thunderbolt.[3]

Preaching on Luke 2:33-40, Luther proclaimed:

> [T]he Gospel assuredly has no worse enemies than those who are exalted, sensible, wise, virtuous, and holy folk. The higher they have risen in such virtues, the bitterer they are against the Gospel, as is evident. The more diligent a monk has been in obedience to his rules and order, the more he has prayed, the more strictly he has fasted, the more furiously does he rage against the Gospel. This certainly is a great calamity and an exceeding terrible situation.[4]

Underscoring that self-righteousness is the ultimate danger before God, Luther, as we have already noted, wrote that "[the] idea of self-righteousness is the bitterest blasphemy against God."[5]

John Calvin spoke much the same way as did Luther about self-righteousness before God. Commenting on words of St. Paul, Calvin observed:

> There is nothing in us but sin; there is nothing in us but corruption; God must needs reject us and hate us; he must needs become our deadly enemy, and utter his vengeance upon us. To be sure we are in the dungeons of hell until God have reached us his hand, and had pity upon us. It is not for any man to exempt himself from this confusion, for from the greatest to the least of us we are all plunged into it. Nor let us boast of the things which we have by nature. For God finds us void of all goodness; we have not one drop of virtue, wisdom, or righteousness, but contrariwise, we are full of corruption; we are ready to burst with filth and uncleanness; we are bond slaves to Satan, under the tyranny and bondage of death; and at a word we are plunged into hell.[6]

Most certainly, reformers of the 16th century spoke of self-righteousness as the worst possible danger before God just as does the Scripture. Self-righteousness blasphemes God and plunges us into hell.

5. Our Greatest Danger Among People

Danger to Ourselves

Our self-righteousness, as long as it dominates our lives, separates us from God. This is the greatest of all dangers. But there are also correlative dangers. Our self-righteousness is also the ultimate danger to ourselves and to our interpersonal relationships. Our self-righteousness is destructive to ourselves and to others and our relationships with them.

First of all, we need to recognize that self-righteous persons endanger themselves. They are their own worst enemy. Martin Luther commented on the dangers of self-righteousness to the self-righteous themselves. In his words recorded above about Joseph's brothers he said that self-righteousness makes people smug and stubborn. In another place, Luther spoke of self-righteousness as an insane idea.[1] Commenting on Isaiah 42:2, Luther wrote, "[T]he self-righteous are most turbulent, because all of them are by nature sad and stern, all of them are ready to pass judgment."[2] Self-righteous persons lose touch with reality and on some level of their inner being suffer extreme pain.

Dr. Howard Clinebell, a Christian clergyman and clinical psychologist, speaks about the inner pain of self-righteous persons. He explains that it is the pain of being perfectionistic, legalistic, and judgmental. It is the pain of distancing themselves from others, being lonely, and lacking joy in life. According to Clinebell, self-righteous persons are known to have deep, largely unidentified, feelings of self-rejection and self-condemnation. He observes that generally they are conformists and have poor self-esteem and feelings of powerlessness.[3] Richard G. Erskine, writing on the topic of shame and self-righteousness, suggests that self-righteous people deny their need for interpersonal relationships.[4] Many suffer from depression, anxiety, obesity, and addictions.

Certainly, people who are smug and stubborn and have insane ideas are not people who live happy and productive lives. People who are lonely, joyless, and filled with conscious or unconscious feelings of self-rejection and self-judgment live lives that are fearful, distorted, drab, and dreary. We will speak more about the inner characteristics of self-righteous persons in future paragraphs. Now we simply want to affirm that the self-righteous are a grave peril to themselves in their daily living among others.

Danger to Others

Self-righteousness endangers others among whom self-righteous persons live. Jesus said of the Pharisees that they neglected their parents and were blind guides who lacked mercy. The Pharisees were certainly a danger to Jesus by promoting His execution. In their presence many people must have felt the pain of their arrogance, pretence, and prideful behavior.

We learn from St. Paul's letter to the Galatians that some persons taught Christians at Galatia that they must observe the Law in order to be saved. Of them St. Paul wrote, "Evidently some people are throwing you into confusion and are trying to pervert the gospel of Christ" (Galatians 1:7). He said to his readers, "Did you receive the Spirit by observing the law, or by believing what you heard? Are you so foolish? After beginning with the Spirit, are you now trying to attain your goal by human effort" (Galatians 3:2-3)? The self-righteous teachers of self-righteousness were hurtful to the Christians in the Galatian congregation. They threatened their very salvation. In turn, they sought to discredit St. Paul and undermine his ministry. This was painful for the apostle.

The situation in the Corinthian congregation was somewhat different. In that congregation according to St. Paul there were arrogant members. They presented themselves as superior to St. Paul. Their behavior disturbed St. Paul and caused painful and disruptive problems for members of the congregation (1 Corinthians 4:18:21).

Likewise in the congregation at Colosse there were haughty teachers who troubled Paul and upset congregation members. St. Paul wrote:

> Do not let anyone who delights in false humility and the worship of angels disqualify you for the prize. Such a person goes into great detail about what he has seen, and his unspiritual mind puffs him up with idle notions. He has lost his connection with the Head, from whom the whole body supported and held together by its ligaments and sinews, grows as God causes it to grow. (Colossians 2:18-19)

In his writings Martin Luther commented that the insane idea of self-righteousness caused the people of Israel to kill all the prophets and even their promised Messiah.[5] When consciences were in the throes of terror and despair, they were unable from their self-

SELF-RIGHTEOUSNESS: OUR GREATEST DANGER

righteous position to bring others comfort and peace.[6] In his Isaiah commentary, as quoted earlier, Luther wrote, "[T]he self-righteous are most turbulent, because all of them are by nature sad and stern, all of them are ready to pass judgment. They measure everything by the standard of their own life and most severely condemn everything else."[7]

Self-righteousness causes people to hurt others; it seriously injures the lives of others. The possibilities are unlimited. Self-righteous people are critical of others who don't agree with their beliefs and personal ethics and harshly judge and condemn them. The self-righteous feel justified in rejecting and abusing other people physically, spiritually, emotionally, and socially. Self-righteous people seek to put people down, use them for their own advantage, and destroy their reputations. They want to control the lives of others and their behavior. They blame others when something goes wrong and haughtily disassociate from them. Often they exhibit passive-aggressive behavior. They appear agreeable but "pull the rug out from under others" when others are not looking. Perhaps they are even more subtle by being paternalistic, condescending, and pedantic. At any rate, the victims of self-righteousness suffer severely at the hands of self-righteous people. Often their position in society is marred, endangered, or destroyed. Their lives are severely impoverished. Goeffrey Peterson suggests that "we may use religious beliefs and practices to maintain and defend our righteous conscience, without recognizing the destructive effect it has on others."[8]

With regard to the influence of self-righteousness on others, Dr. Howard Clinebell, quoted earlier, writes:

Self-righteousness has produced enormous destructiveness in individual lives and in history. Most wars have been fought with self-righteous consciences on both sides. The murders of countless heretics and nonconfronting women as "witches" were done by self-righteous church leaders for reasons they believed ethical and praiseworthy. Even the Nazi leaders claimed to be obeying their consciences in purifying the Aryan race by systematically destroying millions of Jews and other "inferior" persons.[9]

6. Unrecognized by the Self-righteous

Self-righteousness, by virtue of its very nature, is not readily recognized by the self-righteous as operative in their lives. Self-righteous people don't recognize their plight just because they are self-righteous. They see other people as the causes of problems and themselves as the solution to problems. They believe they are always right and that others who do not agree with them are wrong. Thus they do not usually reach out for help to overcome their very dangerous malady. They see no reason to seek help; only others need help from their perspective. They are in denial and incapable by their own reason and strength to do a reality check. This denial is especially true of persons who suffer from all kinds of addictions. Addicted people are usually quite self-righteous and afflict others as well as themselves.

Certainly, the Pharisees did not recognize that they were self-righteous. They truly believed that God loved them because they were so good and that others who were not one of them were inferior to them and cursed by God.

Martin Luther insightfully observed the denial process of the self-righteous. He wrote:

> [T]he ungodly, that is, the self-righteous, insist that the promises apply to them, but the threats to the heretics, that is, the truly godly. Thus that word of the psalm is altogether true: "There is no fear of God before their eyes." And even when they experience some suffering in their body, there is still no fear but boasting that they are being punished for righteousness' sake, not for the sake of their sins.[1]

Likewise, in his Galatians' commentary Luther observed, "[T]he self-righteous, who refrain from sins outwardly and seem to live blameless and religious lives, cannot avoid a presumption of confidence and righteousness which cannot coexist with faith in Christ."[2] Lecturing on Romans, Luther spoke pointedly of the denial of self-righteousness. He said, "Because they [the arrogant heretics and the self-righteous] do not recognize the Law of God against them, it is impossible for them to recognize their sin; therefore they are also incapable of correction."[3]

Self-righteousness is a hazardous phenomenon. Unfortunately, the more self-righteousness we become the more secure and safe we sometimes feel. We are like a man dying in a snow storm. As the snows grows deeper and the more the snow covers him, the warmer and sleepier he becomes. He yearns to stop his struggle to survive and to lie down and sleep. He is truly at the brink of death and will surely die if he does not struggle on toward a safe haven. It is true that as long as we have even the smallest faith we remain in a right relationship with God. But frail faith can quickly become no faith if we do not permit the Holy Spirit to work stronger faith within us through the Word of the Gospel and the Blessed Supper of Our Lord's Body and Blood.

7. Its Origins and Dynamics

Origins of Self-righteousness

What is the source of self-righteousness in human lives? The Scripture gives the answer. The source is our inherited sinful condition. Like David of old, we are sinful from the time our mothers conceived us and at birth (Psalm 51:5). We correctly confess that we are by nature sinful and unclean. As St. Paul declares, we are dead in trespasses and sins (Ephesians 2:1). We are so sinful that we cannot but sin, and our primary sin is pride that is self-righteous and arrogant. We see ourselves as much better than we are before God and among others, and we let God and other people know it by what we say and how we behave.

Actually, our basic pride-sin is that we want to be God. Martin Luther observed, "Pride drives to all sins. The chief sin is the desire to be God. . . ."[1] Bertrand Russell wrote, "Every man would like to be God, if it were possible, some few find it difficult to admit the impossibility."[2] In *Whatever Happened to Sin?* Karl Menninger wrote, "Pride, a virtue under certain circumstances, was—and still is—considered by theologians the basic form of sin.... Synonyms for pride are vanity, egocentricity, hubris, arrogance, self-adoration, selfishness, self-love and narcissism."[3]

The Book of Genesis, chapter 3, tells about the origin of pride that is self-righteous and arrogant. Our first parents, Adam and Eve, were holy and righteous. So that they would continue to be holy and righteous by their own will, God created Adam and Eve able to sin or not to sin. Unfortunately for all people of every age,

Adam and Eve willed to sin by disobeying God when the Evil One tempted them to arrogant pride and self-righteousness. They willed not to obey God but to desire to be like God and possess the knowledge of good and evil. Thinking that they were far too good simply to be the beings God created them to be, out of their new-found pride they ate of the forbidden tree in the midst of the garden in order to be like God knowing good and evil. As Luther commented, "Adam wanted to be God, and God should be nothing."[4]

Everything went wrong that day in the Garden of Eden. Adam and Eve realized that they were naked and, experiencing guilt and fear, they hid from God. Soon Adam, showing his self-righteous attitude before God, blamed Eve for his disobedience and then arrogantly blamed God Himself because He had put the woman in the garden to be with him. Thus we have the origin among human beings of pride that is self-righteous and arrogant. So we, all of us, from the time of Adam and Eve are born sinful and unclean. We are by nature pridefully self-righteous.

Jesus had this to say about the source of self-righteousness and its attendant evils: "What comes out of a man makes him 'unclean.' For from within, out of men's hearts, come evil thoughts, sexual immorality, theft, murder, adultery, greed, malice, arrogance and folly. All these evils come from inside and make a man 'unclean'" (Mark 7:21-23).

Rooted in separation from God from the time of birth, self-righteousness is shaped by many facets of our sinful thought and feeling processes. Dr. Clinebell, as we have previously observed, as well as other counseling professionals, describe self-righteous people as those who suffer unknowingly from the pain of not being accepted as they are, from poor self-esteem, and from deep feelings of self-rejection and self-judgment. At some level of their beings they experience feelings of powerlessness and are afraid of not being in control of life and situations that arise in daily living. People's self-righteousness is the way they try to feel better about themselves, control others, and protect themselves from their negative feelings and destructive impulses. Self-righteous people usually are rigid conformists. Their self-righteousness denies their need for relationships as they alienate themselves from people and people from themselves. These are ways self-righteousness works its evil.

Here are words of Dr. Clinebell that address sinful origins of self-righteousness and as well as the dynamics of self-righteousness discussed in the next section. Speaking in psychological terms, he writes:

> The familiar line, "Some people don't have problems, they are problems!" seems to describe self-righteous people. Actually they also *have* problems of which their self-righteousness is a symptomatic defense. Self-righteousness is a way of trying to reinforce shaky self-esteem by a sense of moral superiority. Feeling one-up on those perceived as ethically and religiously inferior enables such persons to avoid experiencing their deep feelings of self-rejection and self-judgment. Self-righteousness can also be a way of maintaining a sense of power over others—a spouse or children—and of justifying one's attempts to control them. The need for such feelings of power is a defense against hidden feelings of powerlessness and fear of not being in control. Self-righteousness enables persons to avoid

confronting their neurotic guilt and subconscious conflicts about their own sexual and aggressive impulses.[5]

Dynamics of Self-righteousness

Geoffrey Peterson, in his book *Conscience and Caring,* speaks of self-righteousness as a "righteous conscience." He identifies two types of righteous consciences that may be separate or merge into one. The first type of righteous conscience is the conforming conscience. People with this kind of conscience have "a deep need to measure up to the current standards and expectations of their own group. They experience a sense of shame if they depart from the values of that group."[6] These people tend to see evil in people different from themselves.

The second type of righteous conscience that Peterson names is the legalistic conscience. "People with a legalistic conscience adhere to whatever legal or moral code has supreme status and authority. There is again a tendency to look down on people who do not subscribe to the revered code."[7] This kind of conscience, Peterson observes, finds expression in the prayer of the Pharisee in the temple, "God, I thank you that I am not like other men—robbers, evildoers, adulterers—or even like this tax collector" (Luke 18:1-12).

Peterson concludes, "[W]e may use religious beliefs and practices to maintain and defend our righteous conscience, without recognizing the destructive effect it has on others. When our conscience is threatened, we are likely to strengthen our defenses and attack those who threaten us." Peterson goes on to say, "Righteous conscience processes are probably involved in all of us to some degree. The complexity of human beings is such that guilty and righteous feelings can coexist and interact within the same conscience"[8]

One of the dynamics of self-righteousness that I strongly believe needs more elaboration is that of control. The self-righteous can be found everywhere attempting to control the lives of others. They are control-driven. Unwilling or not able to control themselves and their tragic lives of anxiety, insecurity, and hopelessness, they try to find some serenity by frantically attempting to control others according to their will. Those who disagree with the self-righteous are considered by them as wrong, even evil. However, those who follow controllers receive rich rewards for their obedience. When not obeyed, the "control freaks," whether religious or secular, become enraged. The self-righteous are gifted manipulators and punish those who are disobedient to their whims and wishes. Quite likely many of these people misuse such disciplines as assertiveness training to put their control drive into practice.

By way of summary, I want to underscore that, in their relationships with others, people dominated by the righteousness of self seek to lord it over others, to express superiority over others, to fulfill their own self-centered agendas, to meet their own personal needs, to pit people against each other for their own satisfaction, to put people down in order to put themselves up. Often, too, self-righteous persons use their self-righteous posture to hide or minimize their personal behavior they don't want others to know about or take seriously. Mark Twain noted this when he humorously had Huckleberry Finn say, "Pretty soon I wanted to smoke, and asked the widow to let me. But she wouldn't. She said it was a mean practice and wasn't clean, and I must try not to do it anymore . . . And she took snuff too; of course that was all right, because she done it herself."⁹

Part 2

Our Greatest Danger: What God Does About Self-righteousness

8. Shows Us our Need and Inability to Rescue Ourselves From Self-righteousness

What is the greatest thing we need in the face of our ultimate danger? What we need is true righteousness before God that sees us victoriously through life and death and into eternity. We need God's replacement of true righteousness for our deceitful and perilous self-righteousness. However, as we have already discussed, self-righteousness before God comes naturally to all of us. Because we are separated from God and sin is active within us, we inevitably focus on how much God must love us because of who we are, how good we are, and how much good we do. We deny that we are self-righteous and, as might be expected, believe that we are righteous before God. This is the core of our self-righteousness. Self-righteousness tells us that we are not self-righteous.

But there is good news for us, the best of all good news. The good news is this: self-righteousness before God can be replaced with true righteousness before God. God Himself sees to that. This is the truth that St. Paul discusses clearly, persuasively, and at great length in his letter to the Romans.

SELF-RIGHTEOUSNESS: OUR GREATEST DANGER

In order to possess true righteousness before God we need, first of all, to confront the Law that God has given us and that is summarized in the Ten Commandments. This Law is God Himself confronting us with the reality that we, all of us, are unrighteous before Him. Referring to Psalm 14, St. Paul writes, "There is no one righteous, not even one; there is no one who understands, no one who seeks God. All have turned away, they have together become worthless; there is no one who does good, not even one. . . ." (Romans 3:10-12).

If we argue that we do indeed do good, there is some truth in that assertion. Even in our fallen state, we have the capacity to act outwardly for our benefit and the benefit of others, and God rewards us with temporal benefits. Luther wrote:

> Now it is true and undeniable, however, that for himself and by virtue of his own powers a man can accustom himself to decency, respectability, and virtue. One observes this is the case of the heathen. As you see, not all men are murderers, adulterers, fornicators, thieves, wine guzzlers, and loafers; there are many pious and honorable people in the world. These people have splendid, beautiful virtues; they do splendid, beautiful works. . . . Now it is true that God is indeed pleased when men avoid such and other sins and do good. He will not let such conduct go unrewarded. But something different and greater is required to see the kingdom of heaven, namely—a person be born again.[1]

It is most certainly true: whatever civil and temporal good works that non-Christians perform, by making appropriate use of sound reason and the law written on human hearts, do not in any way make them righteous before God. All these acts are tainted with sinfulness stemming from our separation from God. We, all human beings, are sinful and unclean because by nature we are alienated from God and His Life. All too often whatever good we do is done out of fear or the quest for fame. Isaiah declares that "all our righteous acts are like filthy rags" (Isaiah 64:6). What we need to do is take a serious look at God's Law as presented in the Ten Commandments. When we do, it becomes clear that we deserve only God's wrath and displeasure and eternal separation from Him. We certainly do not love God with all our heart, soul, and mind, and we do not love our neighbors as we love ourselves (Matthew 22:37-39). We are not holy as God is holy and as God made us to be holy. St. Paul says it this way: "Now we know that whatever the law says, it says to those who are under the law, so that every mouth may be silenced and the whole world accountable to God. Therefore no one will be declared righteous in his [God's] sight by obeying the law; rather through the law we become conscious of sin" (Romans 3:19-20).

9. Gives Us True Righteousness Before Him

God's Gift

In Romans chapter 3, St. Paul tells us how we are able to be righteous in the sight of God. St. Paul teaches that there is a righteousness that comes from the righteous God that has nothing to do with the law or our attempts to do what the law requires. True righteousness is God's gift. We are declared righteous and just as a gift of God. St. Paul writes:

> This righteousness from God comes through faith in Jesus Christ to all who believe. There is no difference, for all have sinned and fall short of the glory of God, and are justified freely by his grace through the redemption that came by Jesus Christ. God presented him as a sacrifice of atonement, through faith in his blood. . . . Where, then, is boasting? It is excluded. On what principle? On that of observing the law? No, but on that of faith. For we maintain that a man is justified [declared just or counted as righteous] by faith apart from observing the law. (Romans 3:22-25, 27-28)

To help us understand the meaning of the term justification St. Paul gives us the example of Abraham. Of Abraham, St. Paul wrote,

> Consider Abraham: "He believed God, and it was credited to him as righteousness." Understand, then, that all those who believe are children of Abraham. The Scripture foresaw that God would justify the Gentiles by faith, and announced the gospel in advance to Abraham: "All nations will be blessed through you." So those who have faith are blessed

along with Abraham, the man of faith. (Galatians 3:6-9)

Justification means being declared righteous by God. "[Abraham] believed God, and it was credited to him as righteousness." Faith in Jesus is credited to us as righteousness. In turn, to be declared righteous means to be clothed in the righteousness and holiness of Jesus who lived the life of perfect obedience to God and died as the completely holy sacrifice for us. To the Galatians Paul wrote, "For you are all the sons of God through faith in Christ Jesus, for all of you who were baptized into Christ have clothed yourself with Christ" (Galatians 3:26-27).

Other ways of speaking of God's imputation of righteousness to the sinner are to talk about the non-imputation of sin and the forgiveness of sins. Because Jesus is the "sacrifice of atonement," God does not impute sin to those who believe in Jesus. Because the Son of God in His dying on the cross satisfied God's wrath for our sin and, trading places with us, paid the debt we owed God because of our sinfulness and sin, God is able to forgive our sins in full. To the Ephesians St. Paul wrote, "In him [Jesus] we have redemption through his blood, the forgiveness of sin in accordance with the riches of God's grace lavished on us with all wisdom and understanding" (Ephesians 1:7-8).

The Scripture has many splendid ways of presenting the saving work of Christ and the blessings made available to us. Among them are forgiveness of sins, salvation, reconciliation, redemption, atonement, justification, and rescue. They are all facets of the same diamond of God's undeserved love. In this book, because we are dealing with the issue of self-righteousness, we are focusing on the blessing of salvation as the imputed righteousness that God provides for us in Christ.

God's Declaration for Jesus' Sake

Let us concentrate more diligently and extensively on how is it that God can declare us righteous in His sight? There is one way and only one way. God can credit righteousness to us because of Jesus and what Jesus has done for us and for our justification.

God declares us righteous because Jesus, His very own Son, became a man and lived among us for our salvation. In the words of St. Paul quoted above, God can declare us righteous because God presented His sinless Son Jesus as a sacrifice of atonement, as a sacrifice to make good for our sins and to make us one with God. It is because Jesus redeemed us, that is, paid the price to set us free from the guilt and punishment of sin. That price was the shedding of His blood, that is, His dying on the cross on Mount Calvary. Listen closely to the words of St. Paul:

> This righteousness from God comes through faith in Jesus Christ to all who believe. There is no difference, for all have sinned and fall short of the glory of God, and are justified freely by his grace through the redemption that came by Christ Jesus. God presented him as a sacrifice of atonement, through faith in his blood. (Romans 3:22-25)

The resurrection of Jesus from the dead triumphantly proclaims that He successfully accomplished the saving work the Father gave Him to do. As St. Paul writes, "He was delivered over to death for our sins and was raised to life for our justification" (Romans 4:25). Before the Jewish Supreme Court Peter proclaimed, "The God of our Fathers raised Jesus from the dead—whom you had killed by hanging him on a tree. God exalted him to his own right at hand as Prince and Savior that he might give repentance and forgiveness of sins to Israel" (Acts 5:30-31). God declares us righteous because of Jesus who is our once crucified and now risen, victorious, and ever-living Savior and Lord.

We can quote many clear and persuasive words of the Bible to show that Jesus, the righteous Son of God lived among us as a human being, as the God-Man. He lived and died among us as full payment for the debt we owed to God for our sinfulness and sins, for our dreadful unrighteousness. Here are a few of the passages for us to consider.

> Jesus: "[T]he Son of man did not come to be served, but to serve, and to give his life as a ransom of many" (Matthew 20:28).

> Jesus: "For God so loved the world that he gave his one and only Son, that whoever believes in him shall not perish but have eternal life. For God did not send his Son into the world to condemn the world, but to save the world through him" (John 3:16-17).

> St. Paul: "Christ redeemed us from the curse of the law by becoming a curse for us, for it is written: 'Cursed is everyone who is hung on a tree'" (Galatians 3:13).

> St. Paul: "[W]hen the time had fully come, God sent his Son, born of a woman, born under the law,

to redeem those under the law, that we might receive the full rights of sons" (Galatians 4:4-5).

St. Paul: "[G]od was reconciling the world to himself in Christ, not counting men's sins against them. And he has committed to us the message of reconciliation. We are therefore Christ's ambassadors, as though God were making his appeal through us. We implore you on Christ's behalf: Be reconciled to God. God made him who had no sin to be sin for us, so that in him we might become the righteousness of God" (2 Corinthians 5:19-21).

St. John: "But if anyone does sin, we have one who speaks to the Father in our defense—Jesus Christ, the Righteous One. He is the atoning sacrifice for our sins, and not only for ours but also for the sins of the whole world" (1 John 2:1-2).

Writer to the Hebrews: "[Christ] has appeared once for all at the end of the ages to do away with sin by the sacrifice of himself. Just as a man is destined to die once and after that to face judgment, so Christ was sacrificed once to take away the sin of many people. . . ." (Hebrews: 9:26-27).

In summary: In His dying as a man, Jesus, God's own Son, suffered God's wrath for the sins of every human being in every place and in every time. Jesus was sinless; He had no sin to cause Him to suffer. Rather, He was separated from His Father on the cross and allowed by His Father to die as a common criminal, so that God might pardon our sins and put us into a right and eternal relationship with Him. Jesus traded places with us so that we might be clothed in His righteousness. God declares us righteousness because He sees us dressed in the perfect righteousness of Jesus. Martin Luther writes:

> [T]his is a marvelous definition of Christian righteousness: it is a divine imputation or reckoning as righteousness or to righteousness, for the sake of our faith in Christ or for the sake of Christ. . . . Therefore this inestimable gift excels all reason, without any works God reckons and acknowledges as righteous the man who takes hold by faith of His Son who was sent into the world, was born, who suffered, and who was crucified for us.[1]

Obtained Through Faith in Jesus

God has shown us His grace, His undeserved favor. But how do we obtain righteousness before Him? Here again is the answer: God has decided that through faith in Jesus as our Savior, through faith alone, we should receive forgiveness for our sins, be declared righteous in His sight, and live in a right and life-changing relationship with Him now and forever. We appropriate God's gift of righteousness through faith. St. Paul says this clearly: "For it is by grace you have been saved, through faith—and this not from yourselves, it is the gift of God—not by works, so that no one can boast" (Ephesians 2:8-9). These also are St. Paul's words: "But now a righteousness from God, apart from the law has been made known, to which the Law and the Prophets testify. This righteousness of God comes through faith in Jesus Christ to all who believe" (Romans 3:21-22). In turn, St. Paul writes, "[W]e maintain that a man is justified by faith apart from observing the law" Romans: 3:28).

Even more, God Himself actually gives us the faith to trust Jesus as the One who saves us. His Word of grace generates saving faith within us and transforms our lives. St. Paul has told us that "faith comes from hearing the message, and the message is heard through the word of Christ" (Romans 10:17). In another place St. Paul wrote:

> [T]he righteousness that is by faith says, "Do not say in your heart 'Who will ascend into heaven?'" (that is, to bring Christ down) "or 'Who will descend into the deep?'" (that is, to bring Christ up from the dead.) But what does it say? "The word is near you; it is in your mouth and in your heart," that is, the word of faith we are proclaiming: That if you confess with your mouth, "Jesus is Lord," and believe in your heart that God raised him from the dead, you will be saved. For it is with your heart that you believe and are justified, and it is with your mouth that you confess and are saved. (Romans 10:6-10)

Just as God justifies us and renews our lives through the Word of the Gospel, so also He declares us just and transforms our lives through Holy Baptism, the association of His Word with the application of water by which the Holy Spirit is poured out on us to save us. These are the words of St. Paul to Titus that tell us this:

> [W]hen the kindness and love of God our Savior appeared, he saved us, not because of righteous things we had done. But because of his mercy, He saved us through the washing of rebirth and renewal by the Holy Spirit, whom he poured out on us generously through Jesus Christ our Savior, so that, having been justified by his grace, we might be-

come heirs having the hope of eternal life. (Titus 3:4-7)

In the sixteenth century the Church in the West had lost sight of the doctrine of justification through faith and taught justification by works. In those days Dr. Martin Luther was the champion of the Bible teaching of justification through faith. Through his ministry the Bible's teaching of justification through faith was restored to the Church and to us today.

Throughout his ministry Martin Luther wrote many volumes in which he explained and defended the doctrine of justification through faith. An example of his powerful and persuasive words is found in one of his documents called the Smalcald Articles. In Part II, Article 1, Luther wrote:

> The first and chief article is this, that Jesus Christ, our God and Lord, "was put to death for our trespasses and raised again for our justification" (Rom 4:25). He alone is "the Lamb of God, who takes away the sin of the world" (John 1:29). "God has laid upon him the iniquities of us all" (Isa. 53:6). Moreover, "all have sinned," and "they are justified by his grace as a gift, through the redemption which is in Christ Jesus, by his blood" (Rom. 3:23-25).
>
> Inasmuch as this must be believed and cannot be obtained or apprehended by any work, law, or merit, it is clear and certain that such faith alone justifies us, as St. Paul says in Romans 3, "For we hold that a man is justified by faith apart from works of law" (Rom. 3:28), and again, that he

> [God] himself is righteous and "justifies those who have faith in Jesus" (Rom. 3:26).
>
> Nothing in this article can be given up or compromised, even if heaven and earth and things temporal should be destroyed. For as St. Peter says, "There is no other name under heaven given among men by which we must be saved" (Acts 4:17). "And with his stripes we are healed" (Isa. 53:5).[2]

Martin Luther was unyielding in defending the teaching of justification through faith because this is the central teaching of God's Word. He encourages us to cherish this teaching as the true treasure of the church and our true treasure.

Recently I read a sermon that referred to self-righteousness as the worst sin. The author wrote:

> Glendon Harris once said that trying to secure a blessing of God by becoming pure and righteous, or simply thinking of ourselves as already pure and righteous is "like getting into the ring with the tar baby. You deliver what you expect to be the knock-out punch—and all that happens is that your hand sticks fast and the tar baby laughs at you. When you use the other hand to pull away, it also sticks fast. You try to get loose by pushing with your feet, but you end up so completely stuck that you can't move at all. We can resign ourselves to being a part of the tar baby forever, living on its terms and perhaps coming to love the feel and smell of the tar. Or we can accept Christ's offer to do for us what we can't do for ourselves and yield to the solvent which loosens the grip of the tar."[3]

True righteousness before God is obtained by faith and only through faith. True righteousness before God is appropriated by you and me through faith and through faith in Jesus Christ alone.

10. Gives Us True Righteousness Among Others

Characterized by Humility

Self-righteousness before God shows itself in hurtful arrogance and haughtiness in our relationships with others. This is not the way God wants us to be. When God declares us righteous, He begins to transform our lives and replace our self-righteousness among other people with loving humility and humble service. In his letter to the Ephesians, after St. Paul declared that we are saved by God's grace through faith, he wrote that we who are not saved by works but through faith "are God's workmanship, created in Christ Jesus to do good works, which God prepared in advance for us to do" (Ephesians 2:8-10). He reminded the Corinthians that "if anyone is in Christ, he is a new creation" (2 Corinthians 5:17).

St. Paul gives us the meaning of humility in his letter to the Philippians. There he wrote, "Do nothing out of selfish ambition or vain conceit, but in humility consider others better than yourselves. Each of you should look not only to your own interests, but also to the interests of others" (Philippians 2:3-4). Humility is that attitude characterized by considering others better than ourselves and not ourselves better than others. Humility is looking after the interests of others and not just our own interests. It is a matter of unselfish service to others. As Luther observed, "True righteousness has compassion; false righteousness has indignation."[1]

Modeled and Empowered by Jesus

St. Paul gave his readers the ultimate model of humility—Jesus Himself. "Your attitude should be the same as that of Christ Jesus: Who, being in very nature God, did not consider equality with God something to grasped, but made himself nothing, taking the very nature of a servant, being made in human likeness. And being found in appearance as a man, he humbled himself and became obedient to death—even death of a cross" (Philippians 2:5-8)!

Humility is the lack of self-righteous arrogance and pride. It is the attitude of service to others. Some speak of it as "living without strutting" and "walking without wanting to be noticed." It is not pretending to be humble or appearing to be humble while really being proud. Humility has the characteristics of unselfish love, gentleness, compassion, and kindness.

Jesus taught his disciples the meaning of humility. At a dinner on the Thursday before He died Jesus washed and dried His disciples' feet. The Lord and Master performed the task of a servant. Then he explained, "Now that I, your Lord and Teacher, have washed your feet, you also should wash one another's feet. I have set you an example that you should do as I have done for you . . . . Now that you know these things, you will be blessed if you do them" (John 13:14-15, 17). Self-righteousness is to be replaced with humility in our lives. Our self-service is to give way to the service and care of others. We are to be Christ to people about us. We are to live out the Christ in us. This is our great privilege. This spells happiness for us and others, and this is the happiness God wants us to have. He does not leave us mired in the pain and destruction of sinful attitudes and behaviors.

Here is an insightful and thought-provoking quote from a contemporary writer: "Jesus does not preach humility because modesty is becoming. He preaches it because it is the only cure for the deadly pride and arrogance that makes us want to kill each other, whether the murder is as subtle as purging someone from our circle of friends or as bloody as nailing someone to a tree. The only cure is to recognize each other as kin, united by the only one who was ever right."[2]

Jesus Himself, called the Suffering Servant by the prophet Isaiah (Isaiah 53), is the One who empowers us to live humbly. His humble service to us generates humility in us and fruitful lives of service to one another. Speaking of Himself as the Vine and of us the branches, Jesus said, "I am the vine; you are the branches. If a man remains in me and I in him, he will bear much fruit; apart from me you can do nothing" (John 15:5). St. Paul reminds us that God in Christ empowers us for the life of loving care for others in these words: "Be kind and compassionate to one another, forgiving each other, just as in Christ God forgave you. Be imitators of God, therefore, as dearly loved children and live a life of love, just as Christ loved us, and gave himself up for us as a fragrant offering and sacrifice to God" (Ephesians 5:1-2). Every time Jesus lavishes His love on us in Word and Sacrament, He empowers us for humility.

Requires True Self-Esteem

Humility does not mean that we think badly of ourselves and put ourselves down. If we think badly of ourselves, we cannot be humble. We spend our time and energy on trying to feel better about ourselves, and we have nothing to give to others. Truly, we can be humble only when we have good and godly self-esteem. This is the self-esteem that is based on the solid fact that we are children of God, redeemed at great cost by Jesus Christ. We are God's very own, and we are dearly loved by Him. Only when we believe this do we have the motivation and strength humbly to serve others. Recall that Jesus washed His disciples' feet only after remembering "that the Father had put all things under His power, and that he had come from God and was returning to God" (John 13:3). We, in turn, do humble service to others when we know who we are and why, what we are doing and why, and where we are going and why. This knowledge enables us to think well of ourselves and fills us with humility.

Other words of Scripture are helpful here. Jesus taught, "Love your neighbor as yourself" (Mark 12:31). Jesus does not ask us to neglect and abuse ourselves. He suggests that we cannot love our neighbors unless we rightly love ourselves, until we rightly esteem ourselves, as dearly loved children of God. On the other hand, as we have already observed, people who do not think well of themselves, are so needy that they have nothing to give to others. How different it is with people who have Christ in their lives to enable them for humble living!

11. Enables Us to Walk The Path to Righteousness Before God and Among Others

God's Law Calls All People to Repentance (contrition)

There is a way to righteousness before God. There is a path to righteousness before God that God wants us to walk and enables us to walk by the power of the Holy Spirit. First of all, God calls all people to repentance. What does the word "repentance" mean? The Bible and religious writers use the word repentance in different ways. Sometimes repentance means to acknowledge sins and to be deeply sorry for them (Mark 1:15. Acts 24:46-47, Acts 20:21). We speak of this acknowledgment and sorrow as contrition. At other times repentance means both contrition and faith in Christ (Luke 13:5). Some writers use the word repentance in another way. For example, when Luther speaks of contrition and repentance in his *Small Catechism* in discussing Holy Baptism, "What Does Such Baptizing with Water Signify," he uses the word repentance to signify faith in Christ.[1]

Usually, the context in which the word "repentance" is used makes the meaning of the writer clear as in the Bible references above. However, when I use the word "repentance" in this chapter, I will signal how I am using the word by parenthetically using the terms "contrition," "contrition and faith," or "faith."

Self-righteousness, rooted in human sinfulness, is by its very nature extremely difficult to eradicate. It has a firm grip on human beings. This reality spells grave danger for every person, people from all walks of life including religious and civic leaders and heads of religions and nations. To overcome self-righteousness and obtain the righteousness that God credits to us for Jesus' sake, all of us alike need to heed Jesus' call to repentance (contrition). Mark records, "'The time has come,' he [Jesus] said. 'The Kingdom of God is near. Repent and believe the good news'" (Mark 1:15)!

To repent (contrition) requires that we recognize self-righteousness to be our greatest danger and earnestly desire to turn away from self-righteousness and every attendant sin enslaving and destroying our lives. Fortunate for us, God Himself generates the desire within us to turn from sin. He works through the Law, summarized in the Ten Commandments, that exposes our sins and their dire consequences for us today and from now on into eternity.

Unfortunately, it is extremely difficult for some people to hear the condemning message of God's Law because they are so deeply entrenched in self-righteousness. They cannot hear it even though the law written on their hearts clamors for them to hear the truth about themselves; they have distorted or put to silence this law residing in their hearts by nature. What can help them? Sometimes people become willing to surrender their self-righteousness before God when the difficulties of life engulf them. When they are laid low by great pain, they sometimes discover the poverty of their self-righteousness, pay attention to the demanding and condemning voice of the Law, and sense their great need to turn away from their rebellion against God. They have a readiness to look to God for the help, for the saving help they hopefully have heard about from those who have ministered to them. Hence it is, writes Luther, that "God frequently permits a man to fall into or remain in grievous sin so that he may be put to shame in his own eyes and the eyes of all men."[2]

The Gospel Calls for the Faith of Repentance from All People

God calls all people to the fullness of repentance, to both contrition and faith. He calls for a complete turn around of mind concerning how people think about themselves and their relationship with Him. God calls for every contrite person to embrace Jesus Christ in faith for the forgiveness of sins and righteousness before God. Jesus not only called on people to repent (be contrite) but to believe the good news (Mark 1:15).

Then, of course, what God calls for He makes possible through the Gospel. Through the good news about Jesus Christ God creates saving faith in us. Here is a good place for us to quote words of Martin Luther in his explanation to the Third Article of the Apostles' Creed: "I believe that by my own reason or strength I cannot believe in Jesus Christ, my Lord, or come to him. But the Holy Spirit has called me through the Gospel."[3]

God Calls All Christians to the Life of Repentance (contrition and faith)

Self-righteousness not only afflicts people who are not yet Christians. It is a powerful adversary that afflicts Christians. The attitude of self-righteousness seeks every possible opportunity to regain and intensify its foothold in the Christian's life and estrange us from

SELF-RIGHTEOUSNESS: OUR GREATEST DANGER

God. The following two pertinent observations come from the pen of Luther:

> [I]t [self-righteousness] is the most subtle, beautiful, and cunning devil, one which bewitches only the best, the finest people. Most of all, however, he plagues and assails true Christians, and he clings and sticks so tightly that no one can get rid of him as long as we have this flesh. . . . Satan and every godless teacher and human nature cannot bear to have their works condemned. And even those who have the first fruits of the Spirit have a battle on their hands to fight against confidence in their own works. The pest is born right in us. . . . This pest is rooted deeply in us. All the saints labor to purge themselves of it. It is a task befitting the Holy Spirit.[4]

> [T]he ambition that we do not want to be absolutely nothing and do not want to regard Christ as having done everything is lodged forever in the heart. Everlastingly we want a hand in the stew; we want to do so much and to serve God in such a way that He must recognize us, must forgive us our sins, and be gracious to us because of our achievements. And yet this should not and cannot be, for then faith and the entire Christ come to naught. For if Christ alone is to count, and I am to confess this, then I must become modest and say: If Christ does it, then I must not do it; for it will not do to put into my heart confidence in both; one must get out. Either it is Christ, or it is my own doing.[5]

Among those Christians readily afflicted with self-righteousness are those who exercise the Office of the Public Ministry of Word and Sacraments. Among ministers of the church can be found those who think of themselves as elitist churchmen. They have both explicit and implicit ways of sending that kind the message to others. They want to be identified only with those who are considered to be elitists and have little time for others. They seem to know little about humility.

Preaching a sermon on 1 Peter 5:5-11, Martin Luther stated that pride among the clergy is especially harmful and dangerous. He had this to say:

> Pride in the ministry is really and directly against the First Table of the Law. Such proud people as profess to be wise in matters of faith and able to master the Word of God are guilty of truly satanic arrogance against the name and the Word of God. They pompously exalt themselves when perchance they have a gift not possessed by others, considering God Himself and all men of no consequence. For this vice is commonly found in the great, learned, and wise bishops and preachers and in their disciples and followers, especially in those who are promoted while still novices, inexperienced, and untrained. . . . Moreover the greater their gifts, the greater and more injurious is the arrogance of theirs. It also happens frequently in other arts that when a man knows a little of something or is called a doctor, he brags about it and despises others, as though his acquisitions had not been given him by God but had been born with him; wherefore he ought to receive nothing but praise and admiration from everybody. It does not occur to them that they rebel against God with their arrogance and are more likely to fall into the abyss of hell than to expel God from heaven.[6]

SELF-RIGHTEOUSNESS: OUR GREATEST DANGER

Luther's words remind me of the message of a book I used as a text when I taught "Introduction to Pastoral Ministry." In a novel he titled *The Hammer of God,* Bo Giertz, a Swedish Lutheran bishop, wrote about three pastors who lived at different times. These three men were shaped by the attitude of self-righteousness and exhibited self-serving pride. Ultimately, however, through the trials and tribulations of their lives they rejected their self-centered pride and allowed the Spirit of God to work the attitude of humble service for the furtherance of the ministry of the Gospel.[7]

Fortunate for all of us, when we do not heed God's call for repentance (contrition) and when we are in danger of being overcome by self-righteousness, God often steps into our lives to intervene in ways He hopes we will not disregard. To the self-righteous Laodicens, Jesus said, "Those whom I love I rebuke and discipline" (Revelation 3:19). The writer to the Hebrews wrote, "[G]od disciplines us for our good, that we may share in his holiness" (Hebrews 12:10). St. Paul spoke of how God cared for him when he might have possibly become dangerously conceited because of the "surpassingly great revelations" he had received. God gave him "a thorn in the flesh" so that God might make His power perfect in Paul's weakness (2 Corinthians 12:7-10). In the words of the writer to the Hebrews, God's discipline does indeed "produce a harvest of righteousness and peace for those who have been trained by it" (Hebrews 12:11).

Reasons for the Invasion of Self-righteousness into Christian Lives

The most formidable reason self-righteousness continues to hound us is that pride still rears its ugly head in our lives. The sin-power that still resides in us presses us to believe that, by our own power and abilities, we are able to be more than we are and do what earns God's approval. Concerning St. Paul's struggle with pride, Luther wrote:

> Behold the man Paul, splendid in spirit and faith, is in great danger of falling into arrogance of being pleased with himself, of coming before God with his own holiness, and of submitting his own record: So zealously have I labored, suffered, preached, converted people, etc. Therefore there was no way of preventing and resisting this calamity but to burden Paul with a devil who so plagued him that he had to confess continually that he was what he was out of pure grace and not because of any meritorious work. So the opportunity to glory in self was cut off. This, then—that it is bitter and hard to resist this temptation—remains the complaint of all Christians till Judgment Day.[8]

Our lives demonstrate that it is hard, very hard, for us to exclude self-righteousness from our thoughts and actions. In my experience as a parish pastor it was not unusual to hear parishioners say things like "I know everything is okay between God and me because I haven't done the really bad things that other people do," "I believe God loves me because I go to church as often as I can, almost every Sunday," "I know my loved one is in heaven because he/she was a very good person and did a lot of good for others." This kind of talk reflects self-righteousness infiltrating our lives.

The New Testament book of Revelation presents the church in Laodicea as being infiltrated by self-righteousness. Jesus directed these words to be addressed to the church in Laodicea:

> You say, "I am rich; I have acquired wealth and do not need a thing." But you do not realize that you are wretched, pitiful, poor, blind and naked. I counsel you to buy from me gold refined in the fire, so you can become rich; and white clothes to wear, so that you can cover your shameful nakedness; and salve to put on your eyes, so you can see. Those whom I love I rebuke and discipline. So be earnest and repent. (Revelation 3:17-19)

Jesus characterized the Laodiceans as neither hot nor cold but as lukewarm. He said He was about to spit them out of his mouth (Revelation 3:16). What can we learn from this? We can safely conclude that, at least for a time, a degree of self-righteousness and faith can exist side by side. But this co-existence is exceedingly dangerous because, without daily attention to eradicating self-righteousness and strengthening faith, self-righteousness will eradicate faith. This is why Jesus called the Laodiceans to be earnest and repent.

How can we explain the coexistence of self-righteousness and faith for any length of time at all? This is the way it works: When God declares us righteous for Jesus' sake, He endows us with the gift of the Holy Spirit to transform our lives. He does not let us continue to live according to dangerous grandiose delusions, in the misery of slavery to sin, and as people who hurt ourselves and other people and dishonor Him. He begins to renew us to live as the righteous people He has declared us to be, to be what we are. And this we do, but not perfectly, because sin still dwells in parts of our thinking, willing, and feeling not yet influenced by the Spirit of God. Like St. Paul, we acknowledge that we don't always do the good we want to do and often do the evil we don't want to do (Romans 7:14-15).

Self-righteousness is always on the offensive in our lives. We are at the same time forgiven people and sinners. Thus, in His love God continually calls us to repentance (contrition). Then, in His love God, announcing to us the Gospel of Jesus Christ, enables us to add faith in Jesus for true righteousness. He gives us the gift of repentance in its fullest sense (contrition and faith).

There are correlative reasons we should consider that are doors we open for self-righteousness. The Gospel is such good news that we sometimes have trouble believing it is really true. We lose sight of how great God's love and grace really are. We revert back to thinking that we surely can and must have to do something good to deserve or earn God's love. On some level we feel that it can't be true that God forgives our sins and accepts us as we are through faith in Jesus without any merit or worthiness of our part. Surely, we think, there must be something we have to do. Some people say, "If it sounds too good to be true, it probably is." But this is not the case with the good news of God's love and forgiveness. Yes, it does sound too good to be true, but it is true. The Bible is very clear about the message of the Gospel. It leaves us in no doubt.

Another thing to consider: Perhaps the good news of the Gospel is so far removed from our human experience, that it is difficult for us to hear it or understand it. After all, we live in a world that demands and extols self-achievement and rewards us for being and doing good. Without God illuminating us we don't know of any other way of being successful and being approved among others. Thus when God comes along with the message of His unconditional love for us, it is difficult for us even to think in terms of such unusual and extraordinary love. Self-righteousness has its way of trying forcefully to permeate and afflict our lives and sometimes actually does. We can be lured away from the faith but not as long as we say with St. Paul, "What a wretched man I am! Who will rescue me from this body of death? Thanks be to God—through Jesus Christ our Lord" (Romans 7:24-25)!

God Gives Us an Example of Repentance (contrition and faith), Forgiveness, and Renewal through Faith

King David of Old Testament days is a powerful model for all of us to follow as we review how God enabled him to walk the path of righteousness. The king became involved in serious sin. He fell in love with Bathsheba, a woman married to Uriah a solider. Then, quite arrogantly, David had her husband killed in the frontline of a battle so he could marry her. Assuming a self-righteous stance, David did not deal with his sin before God until the prophet Nathan confronted him with the severity of his actions (2 Samuel 12). Then, as he disclosed in Psalm 51, he acknowledged his sin and turned to God humbly confessing his sins and asking God for forgiveness. David wrote that he knew his transgressions and confessed that had done evil in the sight of God. He realized that he had been sinful since the time of his conception and asked for God's mercy. He pleaded, "Have mercy on me, O God, according to your unfailing love; according to your great compassion blot out my transgressions. Wash away all my iniquity and cleanse me from my sin. David went on to say, "[W]ash me and I will be whiter than snow. . . . Hide your face from my sins and blot out all my iniquity." In another Psalm, Psalm 32, David declared that when he confessed his sin, God "forgave the guilt of his sin" (Psalm 32:5). Next, according to Psalm 51, David asked the God who forgave him to create in him a pure heart and restore to him the joy of salvation. As an expression of his renewal, David promised to help others also to return to God (Psalm 51).

King David shows us how to overcome the sins in our lives that separate us from God, also the sin of self-righteousness with all its smugness, pride, and arrogance. We are to acknowledge our sins before God and ask Him for forgiveness for Jesus' sake. We ask God to remove our self-righteousness and replace it with the righteousness of Jesus that He credits to us when, by His grace, we trust in Jesus as the One who died for our sins and rose again. Again, for our salvation God makes all of this possible through His Word of Law and Gospel. We cannot say this too often in praise of God. God works contrition through the Law and faith through the Gospel. If we do not penitently confess our sins and believe in Jesus Christ, it is only because we oppose the gracious work of God. May it never be so!

The Path to the Life of Repentance (contrition and faith) Is the Christian's Daily Return to the Baptismal Font Enabled and Nurtured by the Gospel in Word and Sacrament

Martin Luther reminds us in his *Small Catechism* that the repentance (contrition and faith) path to righteousness before God is the path that leads us and every Christian to return to the Baptismal Font each and every day of our lives. We do not return literally or to be baptized over and over again. Rather, we daily turn to God remembering our baptism when He clothed us with the righteousness of Christ, made of His own, and endowed us with the Holy Spirit to live lives of faith and love. We ask Him to continue to work repentance (contrition and faith) in our lives. Answering the question concerning the significance of Baptism for our daily lives, Luther wrote of Baptism, "It signifies that the old Adam in us, together with all sins and evil lusts, should be drowned by daily sorrow [contrition] and repentance [faith] and be put to death, and that the new man should come forth daily and rise up, cleansed and righteous, to live in God's presence."[9]

Clearly, the Gospel is the power of God at work in us to bring us to the fullness of repentance, which in its fullness is not just sorrow for sin but the turning around from sin to our Savior in faith for forgiveness and new life in Him. Thus God daily uses the Law to convict us of our sins and lead us to Christ. In turn, the Gospel daily announces to us the good news of God's love in Christ and brings us to greater faith. God turns us around by His own power. The Law serves the Gospel and the Gospel generates faith in us by which we abandon our self-righteousness and are declared righteous before God.

In order to escape the terrible danger of self-righteousness, it is imperative for us to take the Law of God seriously when it condemns us to death for our haughty disobedience to God. We need to permit the Law to terrify us and then to be, as St. Paul says, the schoolmaster that brings us to Christ. Next, we need daily to place ourselves under the Gospel of God by treasuring and making use of the good news of His love and forgiveness. The Gospel, and only the Gospel, is the power that brings us to faith and keeps us in the faith. The Gospel is the key to escaping from self-righteousness, the ultimate danger for our lives, and to dealing with those characteristics of our lives that generate and foster self-righteousness.

Embraced by the love of God and defined by God's acceptance in Holy Baptism, we no longer need self-righteousness to reinforce our self-esteem and to avoid feelings of self-judgment and self-rejection. We no longer need to control others to defend ourselves from feelings of powerlessness. In Christ we become new creations (2 Corinthians 5:17). As new creations we are able to learn from our experiences with self-righteousness and cause those experiences to work positively for us and others. This is what St. Paul was doing when he talked about the victory Jesus Christ gave him in dealing with sin that lived in him. St. Paul learned and grew from his encounter with the evil within (Romans 7:14-25). As Horatius Bonar observed, "An unforgiven person is always self-righteous and proud. It is the free, the complete forgiveness of the cross, that humbles the soul and melts the heart."[10] This forgiveness and all its blessings continually come to us richly and daily in the Word of the Gospel that we read, hear, and speak; that created us to be God's possession in the Sacrament of Holy Baptism; and that works in us through the Sacrament of the Lord's Supper.

The Lord's Supper, also called the Holy Communion, the Lord's Table, the Eucharist, and the Sacrament of the Altar, is a vital and essential gift of God to us for our lives of repentance. In His Holy Meal the Lord Jesus gives us, together with bread and wine, His very Body and Blood given and shed for us for the forgiveness of sins. Participation in the Holy Supper within the fellowship of Christians bids us to reach out to Jesus with sorrow for our sins and with faith that embraces His forgiveness so that we receive from Him pardon for our sins, life, and salvation—the gifts we need for a life of continual repentance. Certainly by the gift of His Body and Blood the Lord Jesus assures us of the forgiveness of sins and righteousness before God, the Father. He strengthens our faith and Christian assurance. He enriches our lives with His own life within us and our sharing and caring fellowship with our fellow-members of the Body, the church. Jesus prepares us for, and gives us a foretaste of, the heavenly feast to come. Blessed Martin Luther once said, "For as we eat him [Jesus], he abides in us and we in him. For he is not digested or transformed but ceaselessly transforms us, our soul into righteousness, our body into immortality."[11] He also most comfortingly commented that the sacrament is "a pure, wholesome, soothing medicine, which aids and quickens us in both soul and body. For where the soul is healed, the body has benefited also."[12]

If we should wonder how Jesus can give us His body and Lord in the Eucharist, we do well to review what the Scripture teaches about the presence of the risen, ascended, and exalted Christ. Let us remember: Jesus is both God and man. After He gave his flesh for the life of the world, as the God-man He rose from the dead, and ascended in heaven, and sits at the right hand of God, the Father. Jesus' human nature came to participate fully in the divine power and glory of His divine nature, and thereby, according to His human nature, to participate completely in the Father's glory, power, and cosmic rule. St. Paul provides this testimony,

> [H]e [God] raised him [Christ] from the dead and seated him at his right hand in the heavenly realms, for above all rule and authority, power and dominion, and every title that can be given, not only in the present age but also in the one to come. And God placed all things under his feet and appointed him to be head over everything to the church, which is his body, the fullness of him *who fills everything in every way.* (Ephesians 1:21-23, *my emphasis*)

From Paul's words it is apparent that the right hand of God is everywhere and that Jesus according to both His human and divine natures is everywhere. He can most certainly be for us with specific blessings wherever he chooses. Thus He elects to be for us in the bread and wine with the bestowal of His body and blood given and shed for us for the forgiveness of sins. It is the same (true) body and blood given and shed for us on the cross and now exalted and glorified. We participate in this sacramental meal Sunday by Sunday and on other holy days so that God can perpetuate our lives of repentance (contrition and faith) as we live to His glory and until we enjoy fully the life of the world to come.

The Path to Righteousness Among Others Is the Life of Repentance (contrition and faith)

As we have already affirmed, when God declares us righteous, He begins to enable us for right living. He imparts to us His Holy Spirit to dwell in us. God's goal is to transform our lives so that we live humbly before Him and among others. Luther said it clearly, "To be sure, the righteousness of faith is given without any works. Yet it is given for the purpose of works and for the sake of works, for it is something that is alive and cannot be idle."[13] St Paul teaches that the fruit of the Spirit living in us is "love, joy, peace, patience, kindness, goodness, faithfulness, gentleness and self-control" (Galatians 5:22).

The path to righteousness among others is akin to the path of righteousness before God. It is the path of daily returning to the Font, of daily placing ourselves under the Law and the Gospel so that God daily works repentance (contrition and faith) in us. It is the task and goal of the Law and the Gospel daily to turn us from our sins to greater faith and outfit us for more humble, loving, confident lives.

Living under the messages of the Law and Gospel is a matter of life and death. It is certainly necessary if we are to live humbly among others. Daily repentance that is the path of righteousness before God is the path of righteousness among others. This righteousness in nourished by both Word and Sacrament.

12. Calls Us to Do Reality Checks

To the Christians in Corinth St. Paul wrote, "Examine yourselves to see whether you are in the faith; test yourselves. Do you not realize that Christ Jesus is in you—unless, of course, you fail the test" (2 Corinthians 13:5)?

This entire book provides information for non-Christians to make initial and subsequent reality checks and for Christians to make frequent reality checks. All of us need to examine our lives against the Word and will of God to determine if we are being realistic about our status before God and the way we live among people. To do this requires us to know about self-righteousness, our ultimate danger, and to look fearlessly, thoroughly, and honestly at our lives for the inroads of self-righteousness and its operative presence in our lives. Such a reality check-up done periodically is truly a matter of spiritual life and death. We need periodic physical check-ups. Even more, we need frequent spiritual check-ups.

Why is it necessary for a Christian to do reality checks with reference to self-righteousness? As we have already discovered, it is essential because the inclination toward self-righteousness continues to be active in Christian lives. We who are Christians are both justified and sinners at the same time. Sin still dwells within us. St. Paul described this experience in his life.

> I know that nothing good lives in me, that is, in my sinful nature. For I have the desire to do what is good, but I cannot carry it out. For what I do is not the good I want to do; no, the evil I do not want to

do—this I keep on doing. Now if I do what I do not want to do, it is no longer I who does it, but is sin living in me that does it. . . . What a wretched man I am! Who will rescue me from this body of death? Thanks be to God—through Jesus Christ our Lord! (Romans 7:18-20, 24-25)

Self-righteousness has very subtle ways of influencing us; it seeks to gain complete control over us. It is so easy for us to begin to think that there is something special about us to cause God to love us more than He does others. It is easy for us to think that we are better than other people and that we can treat them as we please and use them for our own advantage. The important thing, we think, is not to be detected as believing that we are worthy of God's love or as superior to others.

Martin Luther has this to say about the sneakiness of self-righteousness in his own life:

> Let anybody try this and he will see and experience how exceedingly hard and bitter a thing it is for a man, who all his life has been mired in his work righteousness, to pull himself out of it and with all his heart rise up through faith in this one Mediator. I myself have now been preaching and cultivating it through reading and writing for almost twenty years and still I feel the old clinging dirt of wanting to deal so with God that I may contribute something, so that he will have to give me his grace in exchange for my holiness. And still I cannot get it into my head that I should surrender myself completely to sheer grace; yet this is what I should and must do. The mercy seat alone must prevail and

remain, because he himself has established it; otherwise no man can come before God.¹

Many years ago, in 1851, J.C Philpot spoke perceptively of our need for frequent spiritual check-ups. He wrote:

> Pharisaism is firmly fixed in the human heart. Deep is the root, broad the stem, wide the branches, but poisonous the fruit of this gigantic tree, planted by pride and unbelief in the soil of human nature.
>
> Self-righteousness is not peculiar to only certain individuals. It is interwoven with our very being. It is the only religion that human nature understands, relishes, or admires.
>
> Again and again must the heart be ploughed up and its corruptions laid bare, to keep down the growth of this pharisaic spirit.²

God exhorts us to do reality checks and by His love moves us to evaluate our spiritual health. He is the One "who works in you to will and to act according to his good purpose" (Philippians 2:13). In the words of Martin Luther, "[T]his monster of one's own righteousness is so formidable that it cannot be sufficiently restrained."³

SELF-RIGHTEOUSNESS: OUR GREATEST DANGER

In closing this chapter, let us call to mind the words of Jesus in His Sermon on the Mount, "For I tell you that unless your righteousness surpasses that of the Pharisees and the teachers of the law, you will certainly not enter the kingdom of heaven" (Matthew 5:25). How wonderful it is that God Himself equips us to do reality checks and imputes to us and all repentant people the righteousness of Jesus Christ.

13. Bids Us to Help Others Overcome Self-righteousness.

Biblical Reflections

If we who are reading this book suffer from self-righteousness either as a Christian or non-Christian, we have taken a look at understandings intended to enable us to identify and overcome the greatest danger in our lives. It is time for a penetrating spiritual check-up, and this is by no means to be the last time.

If we are Christians who are successfully struggling with the issue of self-righteousness, we can become helpful to those who need to join us in the warfare. We can be helpful because we are living by daily repentance to put self-righteousness out of our lives for our benefit and the good of others. Remember that after David confessed his sins to God and received God's forgiveness and life-renewing Spirit, he said, "Then I will teach transgressors your ways, and sinners will turn back to you" (Psalm 51:13). Having been rescued from self-righteousness by God, we are equipped to aid in the rescue of others. To Simon Peter who denied Him, Jesus said, "[W]hen you have turned back, strengthen your brothers" (Luke 22:32). It was after Peter saw his self-righteousness in thinking he could live life on his own without God that Jesus said to him, "Feed my lambs. . . .Take care of my sheep. . . . Feed my sheep" (John 21:15-17).

A primary thing for us to recall is that self-righteousness is a difficult thing to admit and give up. It is rooted in sin and reinforced by many personal aggressive needs that most often go unrecognized.

Among these needs, we have noted, are poor self-esteem, feelings of self-rejection and self-judgment, and the need to control others and defend that control. Self-righteousness keeps us from facing things about ourselves that we don't want to acknowledge. Of the self-righteous conscience, Goeffrey Peterson writes, "Such a conscience can effectively conceal serious doubts about our worthiness and acceptability."[1] We might borrow a term used by Carl Jung and speak of our self-righteousness and all that goes along with it as the "shadow" side of our personalities. Blinded by the dark and insidiously dangerous side of human personality, self-righteous people do not readily turn to anyone for help because they don't recognize any need to be helped. Self-righteousness strongly perpetuates itself and blinds the eyes of the self-righteous to its danger in their lives and how it is destroying their lives and the lives of others. Self-righteousness seeks to convince us of how righteous we are. This, of course, is why the danger of self-righteousness is so grave and treacherous.

Rarely, then, do self-righteous people look for help until they recognize the dangerous dynamics at work in their lives, especially through the experience of extreme suffering. Thus, Howard Clinebell alerts us to the difficulty of helping others to overcome self-righteousness. He comments, as we ourselves have observed, that it is almost impossible for self-righteous persons to recognize their plight until they feel a need for help. Their attitude may change when they "let themselves become aware of the exorbitant price they are paying—in the distancing of others and in their own loneliness and lack of joy. . . ."[2] This is simply saying that self-righteous people may come to their senses when they painfully experience in their lives what the Law of God tells them about the dangers of their self-righteousness. Such pain can have a beneficial effect in promoting the work of God's accusing and condemning Law. But let us stress this: The Law of God does not produce guilt for the sake of people forever feeling guilty; the Law works to produce a realistic sense of guilt that prepares all of us for God's gift of righteousness before Him.

In reaching out to minister to self-righteous persons, we need to put our knowledge of self-righteousness to work in very sensitive ways. Simply denouncing a person's self-righteousness is not likely to help at all. It will probably make that person more defensive. Paul Tournier once observed that often we believe that harshly criticizing a person for his faults will bring him to a better mind so that he will realize his guilt and change his behavior. But Tournier goes on to say that we actually bring about the opposite result and cause the person to become defensive and strengthen his position of self-justification.[3] I personally suggest that denunciation may be used, and may possibly be fruitful, but only as a last resort. When Jesus denounced the Pharisees it was matter of last resort. He had dealt with them patiently and tactfully on many occasions. Would you say this approach was also true of the prophets? (Matthew 9:9-13; 12:1-13; Luke 14; John 3)

To help others, it is wise for us to acknowledge to ourselves the self-righteous attitudes and actions that we still confront within ourselves. It is important that we ourselves are working hard to get rid of them by daily repentance. Jesus once said to His disciples:

> Why do you look at the speck of sawdust in your brother's eye and pay no attention to the plank in your own eye? How can you say to your brother, "Let me take the speck out of your eye," when all the time there is a plank in your own eye? You hypocrite, first take the plank out of your own eye, then you will see clearly to remove the speck from your brother's eye. (Matthew 7:3-5)

Jesus is saying, "First take the plank [the self-righteous judgmental spirit] out of your own eye, then you will see clearly [with a spirit of love] to remove the speck from your brother's eye."

The only truths that can truly change the person with the self-righteous personality are the Law of God and the Gospel of Jesus Christ, the Law working in the service of the saving and life-changing Gospel. However, these messages can do their work only when self-righteous people can really hear them and process them in their minds. Therefore, we need to speak Law and Gospel both carefully and caringly, usually with "I" messages that tell of our own experience of turning away from self-righteousness. We want to aid people in putting down their defenses so that God can change them.

St. Paul offers us very valuable and important advice to advance our task. He tells us the only way to speak if we want to help others by having them hear and think through what we have to say to them. St. Paul has this to say, "[S]peaking the truth in love, we will in all things grow up into him who is the Head, that is, Christ" (Ephesians 4:15). St. Paul tells us that we need to speak the truth of the Law and Gospel to one another, but we are to speak it in love if we want our talk to produce Christian growth through the operation of the Holy Spirit. We create caring and understanding relationships that provide a milieu for God's Word to do its work.

Jesus once said, "Do not judge, and you will not be judged. Do not condemn, and you will not be condemned" (Luke 6:37). Lest we should use Jesus' words as a reason for not caring for others, we need to distinguish between self-righteously judging to condemn a person and identifying sin in another person's life in order to be helpful to that person. Jesus did not mean to stop us from seeing sin in another person and from afterwards seeking to "restore him gently" (Galatians 6:1). He encourages us to recognize faults in one another for the purpose of giving aid and assistance for spiritual health (Matthew 18:15).

Several passages of the New Testament give us guidance:

> "If your brother sins against you, go and show him his fault, just between the two of you. If he listens to you, you have won your brother over" (Matthew 18:15).

> "Brothers, if someone is caught in a sin, you who are spiritual should restore him gently. But watch yourself, or you also may be tempted. Carry each other's burdens, and in this way you will fulfill the Law of Christ" (Galatians 6:1-2).

> "My brothers, if one of you should wander from the truth and someone should bring him back, remember this: Whoever turns a sinner from the error of his way will save him from death, and cover a multitude of sins" (James 5:19-20).

As we have already observed and suggested, it is helpful for us to remember that self-righteous people are usually much more open to examining themselves and making changes when they are suffering physical or emotional pain. Their suffering often causes them to examine their lives. When they do, they may begin to recognize that their assessment of themselves and their lifestyle is lacking and misdirected. They may sense a need for something more than they have and be ready to accept helping words from empathic and caring people. Their suffering presents us with an opportunity we should not ignore or overlook. Luther writes:

> [G]od comes and takes a hand in the matter and lets the proud spirit fall so hard and receive so severe a blow by frequently falling into adultery and at times worse things that he must come to his senses and say: Be quiet, brother, and hold yourself; you are made of the same cloth of which he is made! Thus he then realizes that all of us are made of the same stuff (*ein Kuchen*) and one mule should not venture to call another sack bearer, because we are all born of one flesh.[4]

King David, as we have seen, is a compelling example of a person whose suffering facilitated the abandonment of haughtiness before God even though he had committed adultery and murder. In Psalm 32 David reported his experience and how his suffering moved in the direction of repentance. David wrote:

> When I kept silent, my bones wasted away through my groaning all day long. For day and night your hand was heavy upon me; my strength was sapped as in the heat of summer. Then I acknowledged my sin to you and did not cover up my iniquity, I said, "I will confess my transgressions to the Lord"—and you forgave the guilt of my sin. (Psalm 32:3-5)

We may not always succeed in leading a self-righteousness person down the right path. Or we may not succeed right away. For example, Jesus Himself did not succeed in moving the rich ruler away from his self-righteous stance. When he came asking Jesus what he must do to inherit eternal life, Jesus asked him if he knew the commandments. He replied that he did and had kept them since he was a boy. Then to bring him to realize his inability to earn eternal life, Jesus confronted him ever so caringly. He patiently said to him, "[Y]ou still lack one thing. Sell everything you have and give to the poor, and you will have treasure in heaven." But at Jesus' words "he became very sad, because he was a man of great wealth" and went away (Luke 18:18-23). By this event Jesus shows us that we are to confront others tactfully and lovingly. Jesus certainly did that. But even so, we will not always succeed. But, then, there is the case of the Pharisee Nicodemus. Jesus succeeded with him and Nicodemus surely became a disciple (John 3; 7:52; 19:38-42). God does indeed give successes to our speaking the truth in love. For this speaking He empowers and emboldens us.

Contemporary Illustrations

To illustrate how conversations may take shape between two persons discussing issues that have to do with self-righteousness, I have prepared the dialogues that follow in which one person seeks to be helpful to another person who shows signs of self-righteousness.

SELF-RIGHTEOUSNESS: OUR GREATEST DANGER

A Conversation with a Non-Christian

John, a member of St. Paul Congregation, visits a co-worker who is scheduled for tumor surgery the next day. Kevin, the co-worker, is not a Christian and is known for his arrogance among his fellow workers. He has an "I'm better than you" attitude.

John: Hi, Kevin, how are things going?

Kevin: I guess you know that I am scheduled for surgery tomorrow.

John: Yes, I phoned your wife to see how you are doing and she told me about the scheduled surgery.

Kevin: I'm glad you came by, but I'm really okay, you know.

John: That's good to hear. If I were in your shoes, I think I would feel rather anxious, maybe a little afraid.

Kevin: Oh, I guess I am a little nervous. I've never had an operation before and don't know what to expect. I wonder what the doctors will find and what they will do when they get inside me. But I'll be okay. I can take it, probably much better than most. I'm a pretty tough guy.

John: Well, even if you weren't, I think that would be okay. I think it's okay for you to be a little nervous. I know there are times when I was better off when I paid attention to my inner feelings and depended on others to help me out.

Kevin: You really think it's okay to need the help of others and say so?

John: Yes, I do. And when I had my colon surgery two years ago, I was sure glad to know that God was on my side and have people remind me of His love.

Kevin: Is that right? Well, I guess I think God is on my side, too. I don't know how He could be otherwise. After all, I'm a pretty good guy and do lots of good things to help other people. I'm certainly not as bad as a lot of guys we work with.

John: I can understand why you might feel the way you do about God being in your corner. I feel the same way but for a different reason than you do. There are plenty of times when I feel God owes me something, but when I take a good hard look at myself I really don't find enough good to get God to accept me.

Kevin: Is that right? Where did you get that kind of idea?

John: It's what the Bible, God's Word, teaches. It tells me that, even though I may outwardly do some good things, I am a sinner who has disobeyed God with thoughts, words, and actions. God is holy and I am sinful. I deserve His punishment, and there is nothing I can do that's good enough to deserve or earn His love.

Kevin: I don't know. I think I'm a pretty good person. I'm not ready to put myself down before God or anyone.

John: I think I know a little of how you feel. It's easy for me to think that God is for me because of what a good person I try to be. But, then, I remember that it's okay for me to admit my sins. After all, God already knows them. And, even more, He has done something to take away the punishment I deserve. That's the big message of Christianity—the good news that God sent His Son to pay the debt we owe to God. And this is what Jesus did by dying on the cross forsaken by His Father. And God promises that by trusting Jesus for forgiveness of sins I have become one of God's people. That faith is what keeps me thinking clearly about myself and keeps me going. Maybe you will find this good news helpful to you, especially now. It's for you, too.

Kevin: I hear where you're coming from. I guess I never did really understand what Christians believe. It is good of you to share your faith with me. I'll certainly give a lot of thought to what you said.

John: I'm glad you didn't mind me telling you what's so important to me that I want to be important to you.

Kevin: Don't mind at all.

John: I'm going to remember you in my prayers and ask God to take good care of you and heal you. I'll be back to see you after your surgery. Keep God in mind and trust that He cares for you because of Jesus. Good-bye for now.

Kevin: Good-bye, John. Be sure to come back. You're a good friend, you know

A Conversation Between Christian Friends

Martha and Anne are both members of St. Matthew Church. They have lunch together at a restaurant in their town at least once a month.

Martha: Anne, I've been missing you at church on the last few Sundays.

Anne: It's nice of you to miss me.

Martha: But what's been going on?

Anne: I just haven't been going to church the last few Sundays. Nothing all that unusual has been going on. I just feel that I do enough good things to keep God happy with me so that I don't have to go to church every Sunday.

Martha: I'm not sure what you mean. Tell me some more.

Anne: Well, you know I'm busy doing a lot of good things. I serve as a volunteer at the hospital. I put in hours at the local food pantry. I help my daughter with her son. I pick him up from school on days when I can. When there's a funeral at church I always bring in food for the family meal after the service. On a rather regular basis I visit folks at the nursing home.

Martha: That's really great, Anne, but I'm not sure what that has to do with not worshipping on Sundays.

Anne: Well, I'm usually pretty tired on Sundays after doing a lot of good things and I'm sure I'm in with God without going to church every Sunday because of all the helping things I do. I guess I don't need to do another good thing every Sunday.

Martha: You know, Anne, I'm a little surprised to hear you talk this way. It's almost as though you haven't been to church at all. We've been friends for a long time, and I have to tell you that I'm really concerned. I am concerned that you haven't really heard, or have forgotten, the meaning of the Gospel.

Anne: What do you mean? You really do sound concerned. I thought you would say something more that's positive and encouraging about the good things I do. I know you do a lot of volunteer work yourself.

Martha: Well, Anne, we've been friends for a long time and I'm concerned because you think that the good things you do, also worshipping on Sundays, are things you do to be right with God.

Anne: I'm not sure I understand.

Martha: Well, it's like this. Whenever we've read the Bible's message and heard it taught and preached we have always heard it say that we don't have a right relationship with God because of what we do; we have a right relationship with God only through faith in Jesus. I'm sure that in confirmation class we both memorized the words of St. Paul: "By grace you have been saved, through faith—and this not from yourselves, it is gift of God—not by works, so that no one can boast." St. Paul teaches us that we are right with God only through faith in Jesus who paid for our sins on the cross and not by any goodness we have or good works we do. Our good works are a result of our new relationship with God. If I remember correctly, St. Paul went on to say, "For we are God's workmanship created in Christ Jesus to do good works, which God has prepared in advance for us to do."

Anne: Yes, I do remember memorizing those verses. We were in the same confirmation class. I hate to admit it, but I guess I have kinda gone off the deep end in my thinking. I guess I have gotten a little mixed up.

Martha: Well, I'm sure it's easy for us to get confused. It's easy to forget. Sometimes I forget and that's when I really need to go to church to remember and have God strengthen my faith in Jesus. The Gospel is such strange news to our ears that it's so easy for us to forget what Christianity is all about, to get it upside down.

Anne: You know, it's really good to have a friend like you who will talk straight with me with a lot of love in your voice. I thank you for being such a good friend. I won't forget this conversation. It is will help keep me putting my faith were it ought to be.

Martha: Let me tell you that you mean a lot to me. You have been such a good friend to me in many difficult times.

A Conversation Between Engaged Christians

This is a conversation between Jane and Jim. They are engaged, and plan to be married in a few months.

Jim: Jane, don't you really know how to get things done on time, even ahead of time? You're so unlike me. I get things done on time all the time. If we don't get on with our plans for the reception and sending out invitations, we'll never get married.

SELF-RIGHTEOUSNESS: OUR GREATEST DANGER

Jane: You know, Jim, I'm really hurt by the tone of your voice. What you say may have truth in it, but I'm hurt by the way you say it. You really sound pretty smug and arrogant, like you never do anything wrong. I feel really put down.

Jim: I'm just telling you how it is.

Jane: But I don't feel like you really care about me and that you're trying to work with me to get things done and to get them done on time. You sound so critical. You sound like you are so much better than I am. I guess I've never noticed this about you before.

Jim: I guess I didn't realize how I sounded. Sometimes I do have "an attitude." Guys tell me that at work. Sometimes you have to be that way to get ahead. But I've tried not to be that way with you.

Jane: Jim, I guess it's just as well, so that we can work through this before we get married. I don't want a husband who has a habit of criticizing me and sounding like he is so much better than I am. It hurts. I need a husband who encourages me and helps me when I need help.

Jim: But, you know, I am pretty good at getting things done. I keep organized. Better than most.

Jane: But, Jim, you don't really have to do it at other people's expense? What about helping them to have your skills? Tell them how you do it. That's what I would like, some concerned helpfulness. I know you're good at your work, but I wish you were a bit more gentle.

Jim: I guess you're right. I guess at work I'm really afraid somebody's going to do better than I do and get the promotion and raise. Guess I like to succeed over others and keep them down.

Jane: But, Jim, you are so good at your job you don't really have to feel afraid and compete with others. Just do your good job and help others, too, to do a good job. I'm sure the boss will see what's going on. He will see the competence of the man I love so much.

Jim; I guess you're right. I do so love you, too. I certainly don't want to hurt you. Let's get on together with putting everything together for the big day.

Jane: Let's do it. And I promise I will be a good learner and work to change things about myself I need to change.

Jim: You know, Jane, I don't know if we could have handled this situation as well as we have if we didn't love each other so much and if we didn't know how much God loves us because of Jesus. The Bible is right: we can love each other and others because God loves us. That's what Jesus is all about, right?

Jane: Right!

Conclusion

Now seems the time to ask: Have we achieved the goals of this book presented in the introduction? Has our examination of the Scripture and the insights of Martin Luther and other helping persons, as well as our own involvement in this process, convinced us (or strengthened our conviction) that self-righteousness is truly the greatest danger for us and others—not just a danger but the extreme danger?

I most certainly hope that I have learned more about the dangers of self-righteousness in preparing this book and that you, too, have gained a deeper understanding of life's ultimate danger by reading through the pages of this book. Self-righteousness is indeed the greatest danger that confronts all of us with its menacing face, and it endangers our lives and the lives of others for time and eternity. Yes, we have talked about a very, very serious business. What can be more dangerous than the greatest danger?

Furthermore, I hope that both you and I have gained enduring new insights into the nature of self-righteousness and how it works. I trust that we have examined ourselves for "dangerous self-righteousness" within ourselves and made the commitment to be rid of it. I trust that both you and I have dedicated ourselves to frequent reality checks. Self-righteousness makes our lives so miserable and the lives of others, too, and, again, for time and eternity. Certainly, we do not want self-righteousness to have its way with us. Nor do we want to stand motionless and silent as it destroys the lives of others.

We have every reason to renounce self-righteousness. We have nothing to lose but misery and an eternal future without God and everything to gain because God Himself gives us His own righteousness and makes us His heirs through faith in Jesus who died for us and rose again. Let us undress ourselves of self-righteousness so that God can dress us in the righteousness of Jesus Christ. What can be better than that?

But there is more. The God who clothes us in His righteousness gives us a new outlook and power for life to be good to ourselves and humbly helpful to others who are so very much in need of all that God has to give. Yes, God actually begins to make us righteous—a work that is incomplete now because of sin but one that He will be complete when we dwell with Him in the home He has promised us.

What more can we ask? We have all that we need to live the abundant life. With St. Paul we say,

> If God is for us, who can be against us? He who did not spare his own Son, but gave him up for us all—how will he not also, along with him, graciously give us all things? Who will bring any charge against those whom God has chosen? It is God who justifies. Who is he that condemns? Christ Jesus, who died—more than that, who was raised to life, is at the right hand of God and is also interceding for us. Who shall separate us from the love of Christ?

CONCLUSION

. . . For I am convinced that neither death nor life, neither angels nor demons, neither the present nor the future, nor any powers, neither height nor depth, nor anything else in all creation, will be able to separate us from the love of God that is in Christ Jesus our Lord. (Romans 8:31-35, 38-39)

How wonderful life is when God rids us of our self-righteousness and dresses us up in the righteousness of Jesus, the Christ! By all means, let us help one another to be rid of the greatest danger of our lives and rejoice to be declared righteous before God through faith in Jesus Christ for the abundant life now and a perfect life with God in the world to come.

Appendix

Questions To Promote Focused Reflection and Discussion

(I have prepared the questions below for the purpose of stimulating your thinking about and application of what I have written. My hope is that the questions might generate additional inquiries and expand the scope of your reflections and discussions. They are thought-starters.

Simply as a recommendation, I suggest that you or your group read the book by sections as you choose and then after each selection of choice consider relevant "Questions to Promote Focused Reflection and Discussion." Use questions according to your time and interest.)

Preface

1. What kinds of dangers, other than self-righteousness, would you add to those named in the Preface?

2. What danger, other than self-righteousness, do you view as the most dangerous today in your life? In the USA? In the world?

3. What does the author state as the three purposes of the book?

4. What is the role of "reality checks" in the pursuit of dealing with the greatest danger?

Introduction

1. What is the basic source for the examination of the subject of this book? Why?

2. Why is Dr. Martin Luther important to our discussion of the greatest danger?

3. Would you characterize self-righteousness as the greatest danger? Why or why not?

4. What are some of the words closely associated with self-righteousness? What does each of them mean to you?

Part 1. Our Greatest Danger: What God Says About Self-righteousness

1. A Reality of Life

A Reality Check for the Most Dangerous Reality

1. Why are reality checks necessary with regard to the most dangerous reality?

2. By doing reality checks concerning the greatest danger, what do we seek to discover about our involvement with the extreme danger?

QUESTIONS TO PROMOTE FOCUSED REFLECTION
AND DISCUSSION

A Reality with Identity

1. What is self-righteousness before God?

2. What is self-righteousness among others?

3. How do you view the relationship of pride, self-righteousness, and arrogance?

4. Are there Christian ways to use the word "pride"? Give examples.

Look at the Pharisees

1. Who were the Pharisees?

2. What did the Pharisees believe and teach?

3. How did the Pharisees show the reality of self-righteousness in humans?

4. Why did the Pharisees dislike Jesus?

5. How did the Pharisees demonstrate their hostility toward Jesus?

Jesus Speaks

1. How did Jesus document the reality of self-righteousness in the lives of people?

2. In what ways were the Pharisees hypocrites?

3. How did Jesus illustrate the reality of self-righteousness in His Parable of the Pharisee and Tax Collector?

4. How did Jesus illustrate the reality of self-righteousness in His Parable of the Lost Son?

St. Paul's Convictions

1. How do the words of St. Paul in Romans 10:3 show that self-righteousness is alive and well in human beings?

2. In Romans 3:10-18, how does St. Paul, quoting from the Old Testament, describe the non-righteous nature of all Jews and Gentiles? (You may find it beneficial to put the descriptive words in language you might use today.)

3. How does St. Paul describe our sinful condition in Ephesians 2:1?

4. According to Galatians 5:19-21, what kinds of behavior can we expect from the sinful (non-righteous) nature?

2. A Reality Before God

Pharisaic Attitude

1. In what two directions does self-righteousness face?

2. How do the Parable of the Pharisee and the Tax Collector reveal self-righteousness before God?

QUESTIONS TO PROMOTE FOCUSED REFLECTION AND DISCUSSION

According to St. Paul

1. How do St. Paul's words in Romans 3:20 refer to the reality of self-righteousness before God?

2. How do you understand Galatians 3:10 and 5:4 as referring to self-righteousness before God?

The Witness of Reformers

1. What was Martin Luther's rationale for speaking of the idea of self-righteousness as "the bitterest blasphemy against God"?

2. What was the opinion of John Calvin concerning self-righteousness before God?

3. What do you think that John Wesley meant when he said that many have a "zeal for God," yet have it not "according to knowledge"?

3. A Reality Among People

Pharisaic Examples

1. How did the Pharisees, in their relationship with Jesus, show that self-righteousness directs itself toward others?

2. According to Matthew 15:4-7, how did Pharisees neglect their parents?

3. What did self-righteous Pharisees neglect and by that neglect fail to enhance the lives of others?

Exhibited by Jesus' Disciples

1. How did James and John show self-righteousness among others when they traveled with Jesus through a Samaritan village?

2. How did James and John exemplify self-righteousness in relationship to others by their request to Jesus?

St. Paul's Observations

1. According to Paul's words in Philippians 2:3-4, how do the self-righteous impact the lives of others?

2. According to Paul's words in Romans 12:3 and 12:16, how do the self-righteous exhibit their self-righteous attitudes toward others?

QUESTIONS TO PROMOTE FOCUSED REFLECTION AND DISCUSSION

What Reformers Say

1. In his 1535 preface to his commentary on Galatians, how did Luther illustrate how the insane idea of self-righteousness made its headway among the people of Israel?

2. How would you explain that the kind of people John Calvin describes would be self-righteous among others?

3. How do the words of John Wesley indicate that self-righteous people impact the lives of others?

4. Our Greatest Danger Before God

Teachings of Jesus

1. What, according to Jesus, happens to people who do not give up their self-righteousness?

2. Why was Jesus sudden death to pride, pomposity, and pretence?

St. Paul's Affirmation

1. How is it that self-righteousness is the greatest danger before God with regard to a person's relationship with God?

2. How is it that self-righteousness is the greatest danger with regard to the proclamation of the Gospel?

3. What function of the Law does St. Paul discuss in Romans 3:19-20?

Vigorously Opposed by Reformers

1. How does Martin Luther, in his comments about Joseph's brothers, describe the danger before God of those who are self-righteous?

2. How is it, in the words of John Calvin, that "God must needs reject us and hate us; he must needs become our deadly enemy, and utter his vengeance upon us"?

5. Our Greatest Danger Among People

Danger to Ourselves

1. How does Martin Luther describe the hurt and harm that self-righteous persons do to themselves?

2. How does Dr. Howard Clinebell describe the hurt and harm that self-righteous persons do to themselves?

3. From what kind of maladies do many self-righteous suffer?

QUESTIONS TO PROMOTE FOCUSED REFLECTION
AND DISCUSSION

Danger to Others

1. How did self-righteous persons endanger the members of the congregation in Galatia? How did self-righteous persons endanger the members of the congregation in Colosse?

2. How do self-righteous persons hurt and harm others? Consider my comments and add your own observations.

3. How do you respond to the words of Geoffrey Petersen that "we may use religious beliefs and practices to maintain and defend our righteous conscience, without recognizing the destructive effect it has on others"?

4. How does Howard Clinebell speak of the hurt and pain self-righteous persons inflict on others?

5. What evidences of self-righteousness do you observe on the American scene and on the world scene today?

6. Unrecognized by the Self-righteousness

1. What does it mean that self-righteous people are in denial?

2. How do you explain that self-righteous persons do not recognize their self-righteousness?

3. What message of God do the self-righteous not hear?

4. How do the self-righteous often explain sufferings in their life?

7. Its Origins and Dynamics

Origins of Self-righteousness

1. What is the source of self-righteousness in human lives?

2. What is our primary sin and how does it express itself?

3. What is our basic pride-sin?

4. How do you respond to the Bertrand Russell quote?

5. Why did God create humans able to sin or not to sin?

6. How did the Evil One talk Adam and Eve into disobeying God?

7. What are the first evidences that sinful pride expresses self-righteousness and arrogance?

8. What do Jesus' words in Mark 7:21-23 tell us about the source of self-righteousness and its attendant evils?

9. What are some of the facets of sinful thought and feeling processes that give rise to self-righteousness?

QUESTIONS TO PROMOTE FOCUSED REFLECTION AND DISCUSSION

Dynamics of Self-righteousness

1. What are the two types of religious conscience and how does Geoffrey Peterson distinguish the two?

2 How do you understand Peterson's words, "We may use religious beliefs and practices to maintain and defend our righteous conscience." Can you offer examples of this possibility?

3. How can we understand the issue of control as a significant dynamic of self-righteousness? Can you offer examples of this dynamic at work in human relationships?

4. How do people dominated by the righteousness of self express their position in their relationships with others?

Part 2 – The Ultimate Danger: What God Does About Self-righteousness

8. Shows Us Our Need and Inability to Rescue Ourselves

1. What is the greatest thing we need in the face of our greatest danger?

2. What is the good news God has for us?

3. What do we need first of all in order to possess true righteousness from God?

4. What does the Law of God show us?

5. Can human beings do some good by nature? Explain.

6. Why is the good we do by nature not sufficient for a right relationship with God? How does Isaiah 64:6 apply?

9. God Gives Us True Righteousness Before Him

God's Gift

1. How does Romans 3:22-25, 27-28 teach us that true righteousness is God's gift?

2. How does St. Paul's example of Abraham (Galatians 3:6-9) help us understand the meaning of the term justification?

3. What are some other ways of speaking of God's imputation of righteousness?

4. What are some of the ways by which God speaks of the saving work of Jesus and its blessings?

God's Declaration for Jesus' Sake

1. Who makes it possible for God to declare us righteous, to credit righteousness to us?

2. Who is Jesus?

3. How has Jesus made it possible for God to declare us righteous, to credit righteousness to us? Give careful attention to Romans 3:22-24, Romans 4:25, and Acts 5:30-31.

QUESTIONS TO PROMOTE FOCUSED REFLECTION AND DISCUSSION

3. What do each of the Scripture passages presented teach us about "God's Declaration for Jesus' Sake"? Review and discuss each passage individually and carefully.

4. How do you evaluate the Luther quotation in the last paragraph of this section?

Obtained Through Faith in Jesus

1. Now that Jesus has made true righteousness a possibility for us, how do we obtain this righteousness as our very own? How do the passages in the first paragraph of this section give you a clear answer?

2. Since we cannot by our own reason or strength believe in Jesus, how do we receive the faith to believe? Give careful attention to Romans 10:17 and Romans 10:6-10.

3. What is the role of Baptism in God's giving of His gift of true righteousness?

4. How did Martin Luther defend the doctrine of justification in Smalcald Articles Part II, Article 1?

5. How do you keep from being a "tar baby"?

10. Gives Us True Righteousness Among Others

Characterized by Humility

1. After God declares us righteous in His sight, how does God make it possible for us to be? How does St. Paul express this in Ephesians 2:8-10?

2. What, according to Philippians 2:3-4, is the meaning of humility?

Modeled and Empowered by Jesus

1. What does St. Paul write in Philippians 2:5-8 that presents Jesus as the model of humility?

2. How do you understand humility?

3. How did Jesus teach the meaning of humility on the Thursday night before He died?

4. In John 15:1-8 what does Jesus teach us about how we are enabled to be righteous in the way we live among others?

5. According to Ephesians 5:1-2, how are we to live righteous lives before others? What is our motivation?

Requires True Self-Esteem

1. Why does righteous and humble living require good self-esteem?

2. What is true self-esteem?

QUESTIONS TO PROMOTE FOCUSED REFLECTION
AND DISCUSSION

3. What is our basis for true self-esteem? Consider John 13:3 and the context.

4. How would you interpret Jesus' words, "Love your neighbor as yourself."

11. Enables Us to Walk the Path to Righteousness Before God and Among People.

God's Law Calls for Repentance (contrition) from All People

1. What are different ways in which the Bible and religious writers use the word "repentance"?

2. What do we need to do to overcome self-righteousness and to obtain the righteousness that God credits to us for Jesus' sake?

3. What does repentance (contrition) require?

4. How do we get the desire to be contrite for our sins?

5. What does the Law written on the heart desire to say to the self-righteous person?

6. Why do people fail to heed the message of the Law written on the human heart?

7. What human experiences sometimes help people to hear the message of God's Law?

The Gospel Calls for the Faith of Repentance from All People

1. If the Law calls for sorrow for sins (contrition), what does the Gospel (the good news about Jesus Christ) call for from contrite people?

2. In addition to giving knowledge of the good news about Jesus Christ, what does the Gospel work in people's lives?

3. For repentance to be complete what two components must it include?

4. What are the gifts of faith?

5. In the Greek New Testament repentance often means "get a new mind" or "get a change of mind" or "make a 360 degree turn in your life." How do these ideas relate to full repentance as contrition and faith?

God Calls All Christians to the Life of Repentance (contrition and faith)

1. Why must people who have become Christians through contrition and faith continually live lives of repentance?

2. How does Luther (in the first quote from him in this section) help you to understand the necessity for a life of repentance?

3. How does Luther (in the second quote from him in this section) help you to understand the necessity for a life of repentance?

QUESTIONS TO PROMOTE FOCUSED REFLECTION
AND DISCUSSION

4. According to the Luther (in the third quote from him in this section), what special temptations confront ministers that require them to live lives of daily repentance?

5. How does God often step into our lives to move us to heed His call to repentance?

Reasons for the Invasion of Self-righteousness into Christian lives

1. What role does pride play in the invasion of self-righteousness into Christian lives?

2. When self-righteousness rears its ugly head in the life of the Christian, what are some of the things you might hear the Christian say?

3. What can we learn about the invasion of self-righteousness into Christian lives from the Laodiceans?

4. How can we explain the coexistence of self-righteousness and faith for any length of time at all?

5. What does it mean that we are at the same time forgiven people and sinners? How can this be?

6. What patterns of thought does self-righteousness confront us with and seek to entrap us in as it strives to make inroads into our Christian lives?

7. How do St. Paul's words in Romans 7:24-25 aid us in our struggle with self-righteousness?

God Gives us an Example of Repentance (contrition and faith), Forgiveness, and Renewal through Faith.

1. How is David an example of repentance (contrition and faith)?

2. How is David an example of God's forgiveness?

3. How is David an example of renewal through faith?

The Path to the Life of Repentance (contrition and faith) Is the Christian's Daily Return to the Baptismal Font Enabled and Nurtured by the Gospel in Word and Sacrament.

1. What, according to Martin Luther in his *Small Catechism*, is the path to the life of repentance?

2. How do we daily return to the baptismal font and what do we do there?

3. How is returning the baptismal font both a Law and Gospel experience?

4. What does God work in us through the Law?

5. What does God work in us through the Gospel?

6. How do we place ourselves under the Law so that it might do its work in our lives?

7. How do we place ourselves under the Gospel so that it might do its work in our lives?

8. How does our daily return to the baptismal font radically change our lives?

QUESTIONS TO PROMOTE FOCUSED REFLECTION
AND DISCUSSION

9. What does the Horatius Bonar quote mean for you?

10. What is the role of the Lord's Supper in the Christian's ongoing return to the Baptismal Font?

The Path to Righteousness Among Others Is the Life of Repentance (contrition and faith)

1. When God declares us righteous, what does He begin to work in our lives?

2. What do the words of Martin Luther about faith and works teach you?

3. What is the path of righteousness among others?

4. How does God nourish and sustain our righteous living among others?

12. Calls Us to Do Reality Checks

1. Against what standard do we examine our lives?

2. For what purpose or purposes do we need to evaluate our lives?

3. Why are frequent check-ups necessary? What does it mean that we Christians are justified and sinners at the same time?

4. Does St. Paul's experience have any relevance to your life? Please explain.

5. Why do we say that self-righteousness is subtle and sneaky?

6. Do you think that the words of J. C. Philpot spoken in 1851 apply today? Explain your answer.

7. What motivates us to do regular self-righteousness check-ups?

13. Bids Us to Help Others Overcome Self-Righteousness

Biblical Reflections

1. With regard to self-righteous people, how does God want us to act?

2. What is there about self-righteousness that makes it difficult for us to help people overcome their self-righteousness?

3. When are self-righteous people most likely to be open to help for overcoming self-righteousness? How does this influence our ministry among them?

4. What advice does Paul Tournier give us for ministering to self-righteous people?

QUESTIONS TO PROMOTE FOCUSED REFLECTION AND DISCUSSION

5. What are "I" messages and why is it so important for us to use them in our relationships with self-righteous persons?

6. Why is it important for us "to speak the truth in love"?

7. What messages do we want self-righteous people to hear and think about? Why is this hearing and understanding so important?

Contemporary Illustrations

Are you willing to role play (by reading) the three conversations I have provided and reflect on them in ways you choose? I hope so and encourage you to do so.

Conclusion

1. Have we achieved the goals of this book presented in the introduction?

2. Has our examination of the Scripture and teachers of the Scripture convinced us that self-righteousness is truly the greatest danger for ourselves and others?

3. Have we examined ourselves for "dangerous self-righteousness" and made a commitment to continue prayerfully to confess our sins and regularly receive |God's promised gifts of grace?

4. Are we persuaded of the value of frequent and regular comprehensive reality checks?

5. What great things can we expect from God through the Law and the Gospel?

6. Are we ready to go about life day by day all dressed up in the righteousness of Jesus?

Notes

Part 1

Chapter 2

1. LW 12:338.

2. LW 12:343.

3. LW 17:17.

4. LW 27:14.

5. John Calvin, "Justification by Grace Alone," Fellowship of a Burning Heart Ministry, www.fbhm.org/sola_gratia.htm.

6. John Calvin, "Justification by Grace," Fellowship of a Burning Heart Ministry, www.fbhm.org/sola_gratia.htm.

7. John Wesley, "The Righteousness of Faith," Global Ministries, United Methodist Church, http://gbgm-umchistoryhistory/wesley/sermons/serm-006.stm.

Chapter 3

1. LW 6: 44.

2. LW 27: 146.

3. Samuel Dunn, compil. *The Best of John Calvin* (Grand Rapids: Baker Book House, 1981), 112.

4. John Wesley, "The Deceitfulness of the Human Heart," Wesley Online Center, http://wesley.nnu.edu/john_wesley/sermons/123.htm

Chapter 4

1. J. B. Phillips, *Ring of Truth* (New York: The Macmillan Company, 1967), 86. Reproduced with permission of Palgrave Macmillan.

2. Plass 1274-75:4067.

3. LW 7:360-61.

4. Plass 1275:4068.

5. LW 12:343.

6. Dunn, *John Calvin*, 112

Chapter 5

1. LW 27:246.

2. LW 17:64.

3. Howard Clinebell, *Basic Types of Pastoral Care and Counseling*, revised and enlarged (Nashville: Abingdon Press, 1984), 154. Used by permission.

NOTES

4. Richard G. Erskine," A Gestalt Therapy Approach to Shame and Self-righteousness: Theory and Methods," British Gestalt Journal 4, no. 2 (1995):108.

5. LW 27:14.

6. LW 27:87.

7. LW 17:64.

8. Geoffrey Petersen, *Conscience and Caring* (Philadelphia: Fortress Press, 1982) 58. Reproduced by permission of Augsburg Fortress.

9. Clinebell, *Basic Types*, 154.

Chapter 6

1. LW 16:57.

2. LW 27:14.

3. LW 25:61.

Chapter 7

1. Plass 1273:4062.

2. Bertrand Russell, *Power: A New Social Analysis* (New York: Norton, 1969), 11.

3. Karl Menninger, *Whatever Became of Sin?* (New York: Hawthorn Books, Inc., 1973), 135.

4. Plass 1273:4062.

5. Howard Clinebell, *Basic Types of Pastoral Care and Counseling*, revised and enlarged (Nashville: Abingdon Press, 1984), 153. Used by permission. Richard G. Erskine," A Gestalt Therapy Approach to Shame and Self-righteousness: Theory and Methods," *British Gestalt Journal* 4, no. 2 (1995):1.

6. Geoffrey, Peterson, *Conscience and Caring*, (Philadelphia: Fortress Press, 1982), 57. Reproduced by permission of Augsburg Fortress.

7. Peterson, *Conscience and Caring*, 57.

8. Peterson, *Conscience and Caring*, 58.

9. Samuel L. Clemens, *Huckleberry Finn* (New York: Lancer Books, 1967), 9.

Part 2

Chapter 8

1. Plass 1220-21:3891.

Chapter 9

1. LW 26:233-34.

2. Smalcald Articles, Part II, Article I: "Christ and Faith," 1-5 (Tappert, 292).

3. The Lutheran Church—Missouri Synod, "Our Worst Sins," www.lcms.org/pages/internal.asp?NavID=3057. Used with permission.

NOTES

Chapter 10

1. Plass 1233:3928.

2. Barbara Taylor Brown, "The Evils of Pride and Self-Righteousness," Pulpit.Org., http://www.pulpit.org/articles/theevilsofpride.asp.

Chapter 11

1. Small Catechism, "The Sacrament of Holy Baptism – Fourth," 12 (Tappert, 349).

2. LW 44:45.

3. "The Third Article: Sanctification," 6 (Tappert, 345).

4. Plass 1278-79:4082, 4084.

5. Plass 1278:4080.

6. Plass 1134-35:3626.

7. Bo Giertz, *The Hammer of God* (Minneapolis: Augsburg Publishing House, 1960).

8. Plass 1277:4077.

9. Small Catechism, "The Sacrament of Holy Baptism – Fourth," 12 (Tappert, 349).

10. Horatius Bonar, "The Sin Bearer," Grace Gems, www.gracegems.org/ 23/ 8_2001.htm.

11. LW 37:132.

12. Large Catechism, "The Sacrament of the Altar," 68 (Tappert, 454).

13. Plass 1230:3918.

Chapter 12

1. LW 51:284.

2. J. C. Philpot, "The Lost and Saved," Grace Gems, www.gracegems.org/ 23/ 8_2001.htm.

3. LW 9:104.

Chapter 13

1. Geoffrey, Peterson, *Conscience and Caring*, (Philadelphia: Fortress Press, 1982), 58. Reproduced by permission of Augsburg Fortress.

2. Howard Clinebell, *Basic Types of Pastoral Care and Counseling*, revised and enlarged (Nashville: Abingdon Press, 1984), 154. Used by permission.

3. Paul Tournier, *Guilt and Grace,* (New York: Harper & Row, 1962), 80.

4. Plass 1277:407.

About the Author

The Rev. Charles T. Knippel, Ph.D.

In addition to his 22 years as a parish pastor and 11 years as Associate Professor of Practical Theology at Concordia Seminary, St. Louis, the Rev. Charles T. Knippel, Ph.D. spent nearly 10 years serving in the field of addiction recovery as a chaplain, counselor, and educator. Dr. Knippel received his Ph.D. degree from Saint Louis University, St. Louis, in 1987. He is the author of *The Twelve Steps: The Church's Challenge and Opportunity*, *When Addictions Threaten*, *Freedom from Hurtful Behaviors*, *Joy in the Parish*, and *How to Minister Among Older Adults*, available from Concordia Publishing House.

Charles Knippel *(pron Kinippel)* lives in East Alton, Illinois, with his wife Donna Marie nee Niehaus, a retired registered nurse and nurse educator.